Terry A. Gentille is a professional textile designer whose works have been produced extensively in England, France, and Sweden, as well as in the United States. He has taught at the Parsons School of Design in New York City, and currently teaches at the Rhode Island School of Design.

The Art & Design Series

For beginners, students, and working professionals in both fine and commercial arts, these books offer practical how-to introductions to a variety of areas in contemporary art and design. Each illustrated volume is written by a working artist, a specialist in his or her field, and each concentrates on an individual area—from advertising layout or printmaking to interior design, painting, and cartooning, among others. Each contains information that artists will find useful in the studio, in the classroom, and in the marketplace.

BOOKS IN THE SERIES

PRINTED

TERRY A. GENTILLE

TEXTILES

A guide to creative design fundamentals

A SPECTRUM BOOK   PRENTICE-HALL, INC., Englewood Cliffs, New Jersey 07632

Library of Congress Cataloging in Publication Data

Gentille, Terry A.
 Printed textiles.

   (Art & design series)
   "A Spectrum Book."
   Bibliography: p.
   Includes index.
   1. Textile design.   I. Title.   II. Series
NK9500.G46   1982   667'.38.   82-9152
ISBN 0-13-710657-2   AACR2
ISBN 0-13-710640-8 (pbk.)

THE ART & DESIGN SERIES

10   9   8   7   6   5   4   3   2   1

ISBN 0-13-710657-2

ISBN 0-13-710640-8 {PBK.}

Editorial/production supervision by June Wolfberg
Manufacturing buyer: Cathie Lenard
Page layout and color insert design by Christine Gehring Wolf

This Spectrum Book is available to business and organizations
at a special discount when ordered in large quantities.
For information, contact Prentice-Hall, Inc., General Publishing Division,
Special Sales, Englewood Cliffs, N.J. 07632.

Prentice-Hall International, Inc., *London*
Prentice-Hall of Australia Pty. Limited, *Sydney*
Prentice-Hall of Canada Inc., *Toronto*
Prentice-Hall of India Private Limited, *New Dehli*
Prentice-Hall of Japan, Inc., *Tokyo*
Prentice-Hall of Southeast Asia Pte. Ltd., *Singapore*
Whitehall Books Limited, *Wellington, New Zealand*

To my mother, Beatrice Geneviev Wagner,
and to my talented students,
whose enthusiasm has been
a constant source of inspiration.

Contents

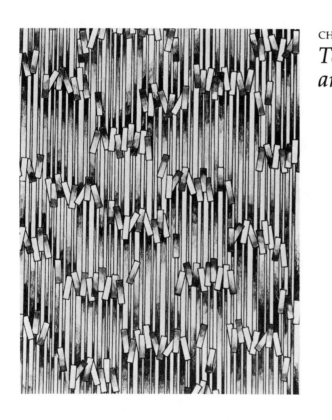

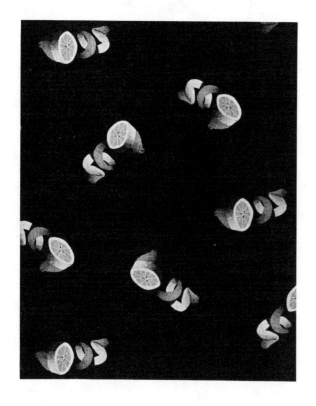

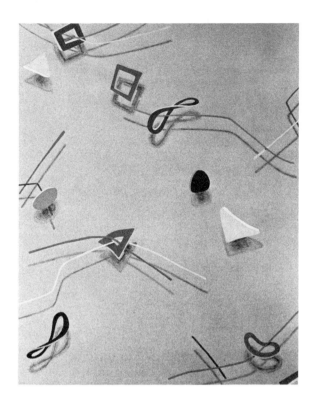

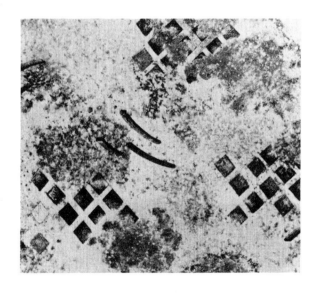

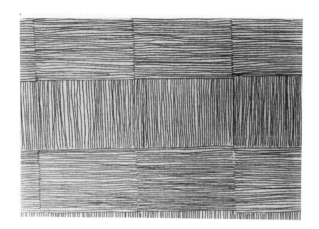

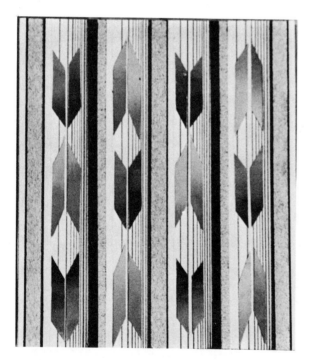

Foreword

In the long history of design, only a small number of designers of flat pattern are known by name. A few are associated by name with particular styles and periods, while others are better known because of their work in other disciplines. Many people are simply unaware that special training is required for an artist to successfully cover a surface with a continuous flat pattern, that such a pattern must conform to a plan, and that a very particular kind of process is involved in the production of a fabric.

All visual artists must be able to control line, form, direction, and color; the designer of continuous flat pattern has the added element of repetition to control. Moreover, the artist who designs fabrics for commercial distribution must be cognizant of the demands of the market, from product use to sales.

The aim of this book is to help students learn how to design textiles. It presents basic information on the use and care of tools of the trade, terms used in the industry, and an introduction to specific production printing techniques. It provides the student with opportunities to experience the process of producing a textile design, from inspiration and concept to final presentation in a form suitable to the requirements of the industry. Exercises are designed to stimulate the imagination, encourage the use of a wide range of techniques and materials, and develop various styles and moods.

More than just a textbook, though, this is a record of a body of work in a contemporary idiom. No one will mistake these fabrics for those produced in another decade. And perhaps most importantly of all, the designs and fabrics in this book are presented as the works of individual artists; for the designers of commercially produced fabrics are all too often anonymous. If the works of individuals are to be recognized in the future, much will depend on the acceptance of commercially produced fabric as a legitimate outlet for the creative energies of the serious artist. Such acceptance is the overriding goal of this book.

Milton Sonday
Curator of Textiles
Cooper-Hewitt Museum
The Smithsonian Institution's
        National Museum of Design
New York City

Preface

This introductory book is directed to the individual who is interested in becoming a creative professional textile designer. While textile designing is an art form, it also has commercial application, offering the artist a means of personal expression as well as a way to earn a living.

Although this book is a guide to *creative* fundamentals, it offers first the technical information the beginning designer will need in order to implement the creative process. It begins with an introduction to the textile industry and a broad overview of the process of turning a design on paper into a printed fabric. It describes in detail the basic painting and drawing techniques used in developing motifs, design layouts, and repeats. A section on professional practices is meant to aid the beginning designer in getting started in the industry.

The book need not necessarily be read in sequence. You may want to begin by reading the chapter on sources of design inspiration before you begin to practice any of the basic techniques; or you may want to learn only one or two basic techniques before you read the chapters on the croquis and the repeat. It is, however, important to have a good understanding of a croquis before you develop a repeat, and Chapters 5 and 6 should be read in sequence. Otherwise the way in which you use this book can be dictated solely by your own needs.

This book has grown out of my experience in the field, my own artistic search for expressive fabric design, and classes I have taught at the Rhode Island School of Design and Parsons School of Design in New York. It is my sincere hope that it will serve to help the beginner, interest the professional, and encourage the development of creative design in all areas of printed textiles.

ACKNOWLEDGMENTS

My sincere thanks to the many designers who allowed me to photograph their work for use in this book. I would also like to thank Patricia Green and Lori DiTieri at Groundworks, Inc.; Harriet Sawyer and JoAnn Kriskowski at New Wave Fabrics Ltd.; Carolyn Ray at Carolyn Ray; the Sublistatic Corporation of America; Cranston Print Works Company; and Mr. Conditti Ltd., New York.

Special thanks go to Regina Ortenzi, Jason Pollen, Maria Tulokas, and Milton Sonday for reading the manuscript and offering me much helpful criticism. My thanks to Charles Anthony Cato for photographic assistance, and to P. Emanuel Clemons for typing the manuscript.

Thanks also go to my editor, Mary Kennan, at Prentice-Hall, Inc., for her generous help, and to June Wolfberg, my production editor.

Figure 0.1
JENNIFER S. ORKIN
Ornamental Transparencies (croquis, gouache, 15½" × 19").
Copyright © 1981, Jennifer S. Orkin.

Introduction

Human beings have always had a profound passion for decoration. Throughout history, art has served as both a means of decoration and individual expression, as people have sought to adorn themselves and the surfaces surrounding them.

Like other visual art forms, the designing of printed textiles for production yardage confronts the artist/designer with three challenges: the technical, the aesthetic, and the expressive. Creative textile designers must be aware of the aesthetic considerations—color, line, composition, form, and shape—as well as the technical processes necessary for expressing their ideas on paper and cloth. There must also exist the knowledge that this art form is not limited to surface decoration but can ultimately become a means of individual and personal expression.

For some it may be difficult to accept the idea that textile design, especially design for production yardage, can be art. We are more accustomed to thinking about paintings and sculpture in these terms. But art takes many forms and is created in diverse ways. In every discipline can be found examples that meet the criteria that distinguish art—as well as examples that do not. Not all printed fabric is art; neither is all sculpture or painting. How then do we decide whether a work is or is not art?

The twentieth century has shown us that art cannot be limited to a particular medium or format. We have understood from it that artists can create outstanding examples of expressive work in many disciplines and media. We know too that art can be functional, as the best examples of architecture will confirm.

If, then, it is possible to consider objects as disparate as a painting, a statue, a yard of fabric, and an office building as having the potential for being works of art, what are the qualifying factors possessed by all? The common denominator is that each is a communication of the human experience, interpreted by an artist in an individual and personal way. Art is a product of the creative process.

It is also relevant that the aesthetic impact of a work of art can be determined in part by the artist's ability to control a particular technique or material. But in visual arts such as painting and sculpture, the work is finalized and completed by the artist. There are no production stages waiting to transform

the work. For the industrial textile designer, the painted and drawn design is only the first in a long series of intermediate stages. A design cannot be considered completed until it appears on the fabric. The textile designer must therefore develop a faculty other visual artists rarely need: the ability to envision how the finished sketch will look when converted into its final form: the printed cloth.

Designs are printed to beautify, add interest, and give variety to the cloth's surface. In many instances they are created to give the cloth more marketing appeal. When considering the completed textile, the designer must take into account all the elements that come together to enhance its entirety: the design of the print, the quality of printing and engraving, the construction of the fabric, the fabric's weave and the type of yarn from which the fabric is woven, and the fabric's chemical finish.

Textile designs are printed on a variety of different fabrics and used for various purposes. We are in constant contact with them in one form or another. They cover our bodies as clothing, our windows as draperies, and our furniture as upholstery. They are made into wall coverings and we sleep between them on our sheets. Whether we are aware of it or not, we are close to printed textiles throughout our lives.

For most of us our knowledge of textile design is based solely on those fabrics that we see around us. This is probably the factor most responsible for the preconceptions many beginning designers have about what a textile design should look like—preconceptions which are naturally very limiting to a beginning designer's work. Textile designs do not have to be based on flowers, paisleys, or fruit. Today many traditional approaches to design layout and imagery are being challenged. The old rules are being broken. The possibilities can be as unlimited as the designer's own imagination.

Creative design emanates from individuals who are genuinely interested in design for its own sake. Designing for some becomes a passion—a passion to develop innovative images animated by creative ingenuity. The development of images for printed textiles becomes, for these artists, an art form and a means of personal expression. They explore its innovative potential and hope to create designs that have never been seen printed on the surface of cloth. Such designers hold a new vision about what textile design is and can be. They strive to make that vision a reality.

Figure 0.2
GRACE DUNKAS
Geometric Series: I (croquis, gouache and pencil, 26″ × 39″).
Copyright © 1980, Grace Dunkas

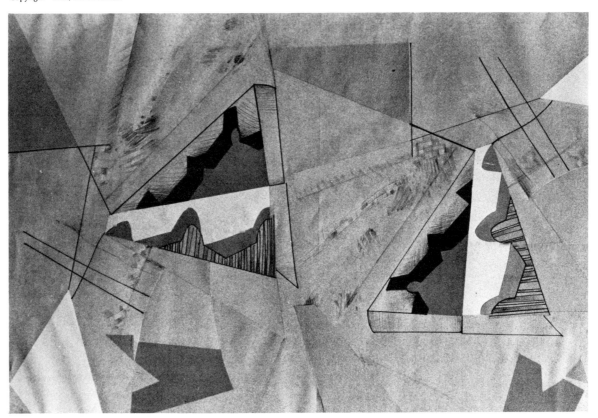

PRINTED
TEXTILES

The process of transforming a design that is on paper into a piece of printed fabric takes place in several stages requiring the efforts and cooperation of a number of individuals. The route to completion is not always the same; it may vary depending upon a variety of considerations, both practical and artistic. Before you begin to create your first designs, it may be useful to have a general understanding of the textile industry and what it does.

THE INDUSTRY

The vast textile industry contains many areas of specialization: It includes the designing and printing of textiles, the designing and production of woven fabrics, the production of base cloths (greige goods) and industrial fabrics, as well as the production and development of natural and synthetic fibers.

As designers, our concern is with that

CHAPTER ONE

Paper to printed textile

area of the industry that produces printed fabrics, specifically yardage. There are other areas of textile printing besides yardage: Domestics such as sheets, towels, and tablecloths, and other flat surfaces, such as wallpaper, are also printed. But the design considerations for these are similar to those for printed yardage. If the designer understands production yardage, the same creative ideas can be applied to other areas of surface design.

The printed textile industry is divided into two major areas: apparel, which produces fabrics for men's, women's and children's clothing; and furnishing, which produces yardage for upholstery and drapery. The industry encompasses many firms of different sizes, each gearing its products toward specific segments of the market.

There are large textile conglomerates, for which printed fabrics are just one area of their operation; such companies may have many divisions, producing fabrics for both

Figure 1.1
ELEANOR R. COWEN
Narragansett Bay (croquis, oil pastel, 16½″ × 20″).

Figure 1.2
DEBORAH BARONAS
Amazonica (croquis, gouache, 18¾″ × 11″).

major markets, with prices from low to high. There are medium-size houses which usually choose to concentrate on either furnishings or apparel; they might also direct their fabric specifically to one price range. Then there are specialty houses which produce printed fabrics for an exclusive market. (This type of firm is more common in the furnishings area, but can be found in apparel as well.)

Among the various companies are diverse attitudes and approaches to developing printed cloth. The printing method, quality of printing, number of colors in a design, and base cloth used will vary from one company to another. Each of these elements is largely determined by the area of the market to which the fabric will be sold and the final price of the completed cloth—the price determining the market, and vice versa.

In the development of high-priced fabrics for the exclusive high-fashion apparel and furnishings markets, excellence of result is emphasized over considerations of price. Many colors may be used in a design, and superb base cloths and printing techniques will be employed to produce the finest quality fabrics money can buy.

Fabrics for mass-market consumption are developed with price considerations taking precedence. Cheaper base cloths, faster printing methods, and limited numbers of colors may be used. Here the goal is to achieve the best possible product within a given price range.

FROM CROQUIS TO CLOTH

The design for a printed textile is usually conceived on paper. The sketch, or *croquis*, can be painted or drawn using a variety of techniques and media. But however executed, the croquis should contain all elements of the design and represent accurately the way the designer wants the image to look when printed on cloth.

The design elements that comprise the croquis will eventually be repeated over the entire surface of the cloth. The croquis must therefore be converted into a repeating design, called an *engraving sketch*. In this sketch, the croquis is organized into units that recur at constant intervals. The engraving sketch is often simply referred to as "the repeat."

The engraving sketch goes next to the printing mill where it is given to the engraving studio for color separation. This means that all of the elements of each color will be copied, in dark opaque ink, onto a single acetate sheet. If, for example, the design has five colors, there will be five acetate sheets. Color separation is a delicate process, generally done by hand, and the success or failure of the design may lie in the ability of the separation artist to interpret the engraving sketch accurately.

After the separate sheets of acetate are checked for errors, they are extended onto large sheets of film. These sheets of film, which are equal to the full size of the screen or roller, are used to engrave the copper roller—for roller printing—or to transfer the pattern onto a rotary screen—for screen printing.

A design is usually rendered in a series of different colorings which, when printed, are called *colorways*. Before the design goes into production, a sample, or *strike-off*, is made of the first printed fabric in each colorway, so that the manufacturer or converter can check for accuracy of engraving and color.

Once the strike-offs have been approved by the converter, the design is ready for production. The raw fabric, or *greige goods*, have been prepared by the mill to meet the manufacturer's or converter's specifications. This entails bleaching the cloth for whiteness and shrinking it to the proper width. It may also include mercerizing and dyeing the fabric a background shade prior to the actual printing.

The prepared cloth and the printing machines are now ready to come together to produce the final product. The printing of the cloth is generally supervised by a designer or stylist employed by the converter or manufacturer. At the mill, the stylist checks printed patches of the cloth to see that the rollers or screens are properly fitted and confirm that the color on the cloth is accurately matched to that of the painted colorings. Adjustments may be needed on several patches before the cloth is finally approved for the production run.

Now the cloth is *finished*, which may include brushing, glazing, heat-setting, or a variety of chemical processes that change the look and feel of the fabric. It is then delivered to the customer.

It should be obvious then that, although the most creative work in the production of a printed textile may occur at the design stage, the ultimate success of the fabric is dependent upon the successful completion of each intervening stage in the process. To this end, the artist must develop the technical awareness and facility to convey design ideas that can appropriately and correctly be realized on cloth.

Figure 1.3
JENNIFER S. ORKIN
Untitled (croquis, gouache, 11½″ × 10½″).
Copyright © 1980, Jennifer S. Orkin

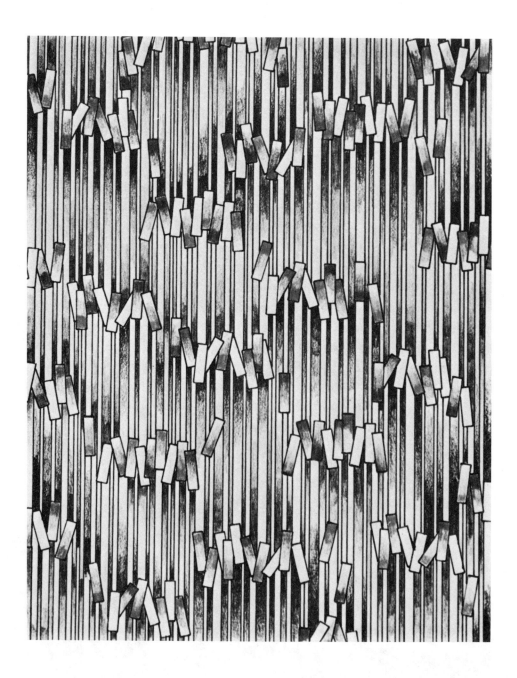

The designer of printed textiles needs an assortment of tools and materials to execute the various designing techniques used in the profession. Some of these tools are illustrated and listed here. It is not essential for a beginning designer to have everything listed before starting. Certain tools or materials are used for specific purposes and can be purchased as needed. The basic supplies are used for a variety of techniques. You will need these and the layout supplies to begin. Other supplies are listed under the technique for which they are used and can be purchased as needed.

CHAPTER TWO

Tools, materials, and workspace

BASIC SUPPLIES

Designers' Gouache—a water-based, opaque paint mixed with a gum preparation. Invest in the best quality gouache; it gives the best results. Good colors to start with are brilliant yellow, ultra-marine, spectrum red, alizarin crimson, spectrum violet, sky blue, brilliant green, burnt umber, jet black. These paints can be used straight from the tube or mixed with each other and/or poster white to obtain a number of colors.

White Poster-Paint—a high quality poster-paint can be used instead of white gouache. It is less expensive and mixes well with gouache colors. White is the pigment most frequently used.

Plastic Squeeze-Bottles—two eight-ounce bottles with small nozzles: one to hold clean water and the other to hold white poster paint. With these, water and paint can be squeezed into palette without contamination from colors being mixed.

Mixing Palette—disposable plastic palette with thirty wells that can be washed and reused.

Paper Cups or *Small Plastic Cups with Lids* (optional)—used instead of palette when mixing large amounts of color for painting a ground.

Sable Brushes—Nos. 2 and 5 to start. Top quality designers' brushes are a good investment. They last longer and are important to good technique.

Camel Brush (optional)—Less expensive than sable, a 1½-inch wide brush is needed for painting color grounds.

Mixing Brush—an inexpensive brush for mixing saves unnecessary wear on good sable brushes.

Bristol Board—two ply with a vellum finish: a good beginning paper for technique practice and designing, available in pads of various sizes and in single sheets. A pad of 11 × 14 inches is recommended to start. The size of paper

Figure 2.1
Pictured are some of the basic supplies you will need, including brushes, paints, mechanical pencil and sharpener, palette, and kneaded eraser.

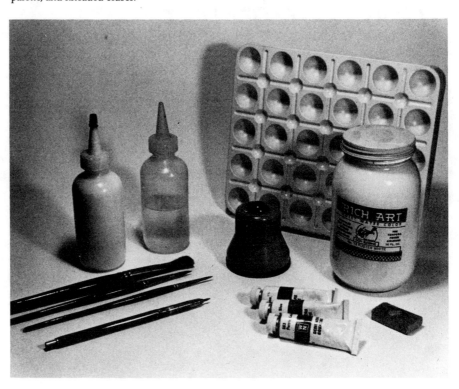

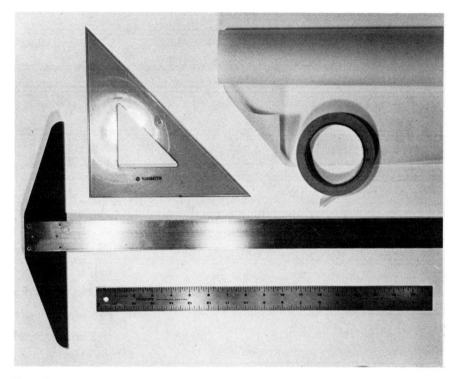

Figure 2.2
Pictured are some of the layout supplies you will need, including T-square, triangle, tracing paper, and masking tape.

you design on is determined by the scale of your motifs and layout.

Pencil—a mechanical pencil (lead holder) is preferable; 2B lead (soft) is generally used; 4H (hard) lead is recommended for detailed or fine work. Wood and graphite pencils can be used if desired.

Pencil Sharpener—lead pointer for mechanical pencil. Electric pencil sharpener is excellent for wood and graphite pencils.

Kneaded Eraser—one that cleans well and is soft and pliable; especially good for cleaning delicate areas.

Two Jars of Water—used for cleaning brushes and tools.

Paper Towels—an absolute necessity.

LAYOUT SUPPLIES

Tracing Paper—a medium-weight, semi-transparent paper; comes on a roll or in pads of various sizes. A small roll is good to start.

Masking Tape—another necessity.

Metal Teaspoon—used for rub-downs or burnishing.

Ruler—an 18-inch metal one is best.

REPEAT SUPPLIES

T-Square—a 24-inch metal one is best.

Plastic Triangle—with a beveled edge, 12-inch hypotenuse or larger.

11

Drawing Board—a wooden board with an aluminum edge, used with T-square and triangle for accuracy in squaring repeat work. Boards come in several sizes. Get one large enough to meet your needs: 24 × 36 inches is suggested.

Drafting Table—basically a drawing board on adjustable legs with tilt top, an excellent alternative to the drawing board. The drafting table is used by most professionals as a working surface for designing and doing repeat layouts.

STIPPLING SUPPLIES

Toothbrush—three or four inexpensive, medium-grade brushes.

Metal Butter Knife—typical kitchen variety is fine.

X-Acto Knife—No. 3001 with No. 11 blades.

Colored Paper (optional)—construction paper or charcoal paper in a variety of colors.

RULING-PEN SUPPLIES

Ruling Pen—used with gouache to make lines of even widths. The broad ruling pen with a 5/16 × 2¾-inch plastic handle is best.

Drawing Compass—used for drawing circles and arcs. May also be converted to dividers for measuring. Be sure the compass has a pen and divider point attachment.

Figure 2.3
The ruling pen and drawing compass with pen attachment.

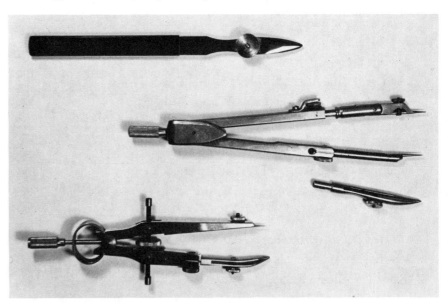

FRISKET SUPPLIES

Liquid Mask Frisket—a one-ounce bottle. A liquid mask used to block out or resist color in desired areas. Dries waterproof but can be thinned with water when wet.

Rubber Cement—can be used as frisket resist for areas of bold design.

Rubber Cement Thinner—for rubber cement that becomes too thick.

Liquid Watercolor—three or more small bottles of color.

SHADED-PENCIL SUPPLIES

Color Pencils—a set with several colors.

FLUSH-JOINING SUPPLIES

X-Acto Knife—No. 3001 with No. 11 blades.

Clear Tape—"magic" type is best.

CARE OF SUPPLIES

Tools and materials properly cared for will work better and last longer. It is essential to clean and store them correctly when not in use. Here are some suggestions about the care of specific supplies.

Brushes

Always buy the best quality sable brush you can find. Check that the brush always holds a point by wetting and shaping the hairs of the brush.

First hold the brush by its handle in one hand. With the other hand, place the wetted sable bristles lightly between the thumb and forefinger. Start at the metal rim and pull gently through your fingers to the tip. You may need to do this two or three times, rotating the brush slightly each time. If the brush maintains a point it has passed the first half of the test. (The exception to this rule is, of course, a flat brush, which would never have a point. Flat brushes should be checked for body.)

Next check to be sure that the brush has body. Press the wetted bristles against the palm of your hand as if you were going to paint. Hold for a second and release. If the bristles bounce back as before, and maintain a point, you've got a good brush. If they remain bent and out of shape, the brush is no good. Keep looking.

Once you've found the right brush, it is important to maintain it. Always wash brushes thoroughly in clean water after use. Gently wipe off excess water with clean paper towels. Never allow paint to dry and harden in the bristles. Store brushes upright in a jar. There should be enough space for bristles to stand without touching the side of the jar or other brushes.

If you transport brushes for even a short distance, they should be packed to prevent damage of bristles. Fold a piece of bristol board in half to make a folder. Place brush inside folder (center back) and tape handle in two places. Close folder and tape shut. Brushes can now be carried without damage.

Squeeze-bottles of white poster-paint should likewise be capped when not in use. Always shake well before using.

Paint

Replace caps on tubes of gouache immediately after use. Gouache dries quickly. If you have a mixed color that you want to keep, add a drop of clean water and cover palette securely with masking tape or tin foil. Color should last two or three days without drying.

Ruling Pen and Compass Attachments

Your ruling pen, compass, and attachments should be completely cleaned of ink or gouache and dried with a paper towel. They are sold in a plastic case, and should always be stored in it.

Figure 2.4
A typical work area.

SETTING UP A WORKSPACE

Setting up a workspace is fairly easy. You can, after all, do your designing on just about any flat surface. Certain conditions will, however, create a better and more enjoyable work area.

If at all possible, your work area should be near a window with plenty of light. Additional light is usually still necessary, though, and there are a variety of adjustable lamps that can be clamped to the table. In general, lighting should be arranged so that your hand does not cast a shadow on the work.

A taboret with drawer space in which to keep your tools and supplies will help keep you organized. It is much easier to design if everything is at your fingertips and you don't have to spend time searching for things you need. The filing cabinet shown in Figure 2.4 works well. The large file drawer is used for storing reference materials. Larger tools, such as T-squares, can be hung on the wall.

You will also need a place to store finished work and large sheets of paper. A heavy cardboard portfolio with cloth flaps and tie ribbons on three sides serves this purpose very well (Figure 2.5). And a fishing tackle box with swing-up tray makes an excellent portable carrier for supplies.

Figure 2.5
A heavy cardboard portfolio used for storing and transporting designs.

In this chapter you will encounter the basic techniques of textile designing. Each technique has a characteristic or quality unique unto itself. Each is used for a different purpose and to achieve a different effect.

Good technique can be defined as the ability of the designer to control a medium to produce a desired effect and to reproduce that effect consistently. Good technical skills are essential to good design; although your creativity is not dependent upon your technical facility, you will need good technique if you are to fully realize your ideas on paper.

Once you have mastered the fundamental skills presented here, you may want to go on to explore other uses of a given tool or

CHAPTER THREE

Basic techniques

medium. A ruling pen, for instance, can be used without a ruler to make a curved line. Gouache, as well as being flat, can be thinned with water and used similarly to water color to show light-to-dark gradations of a single color. Frisket can be combined with other tools and methods to create a variety of interesting design concepts.

It is important to experiment and explore. The techniques herein described will certainly provide a beginning. Through their use, adaptation, and combination, you will be able to create many interesting design concepts. But you should always be on the look-out for other tools or media that might serve you in developing your ideas.

Three steps in painting a shape by using
the flat gouache technique.

Figure 3.1A

Figure 3.1B

Figure 3.1C

18

FLAT GOUACHE TECHNIQUE

TOOLS AND MATERIALS NEEDED:
BASIC SUPPLIES

Flat gouache is one of the most frequently used techniques in the development of design concepts for printed textiles. Gouache is probably used more than any other medium, because such a variety of different effects can be obtained, depending on the tool and the way in which the paint is applied.

The rendering of gouache in a flat manner is one of the most difficult techniques to master. It takes time and practice; but like riding a bicycle, once you've learned to do it properly, it's easy from that point on.

The flat gouache technique will be mastered more quickly if your brushes are clean and of good quality. You should also use the best quality gouache and be sure that it is properly mixed with a less expensive mixing brush.

To begin, prepare the gouache by squeezing a small amount of any color into the plastic mixing palette. If you want to change the color you can combine small amounts from two or more tubes. For the novice it is often easier to achieve a flat painted surface when white has been added to the gouache. Squeeze some poster-white into the well and mix thoroughly (this will also lighten the color). If paint appears too thick, add water sparingly, a few drops at a time, until you have reached the consistency of melted ice cream. It may take only a little water to bring paint to this consistency. (Keep water and poster-white handy in plastic squeeze-bottles.)

Mixing your paint to the right consistency is critical to successful flat gouache technique. Paint that is too thick will be diffi-cult to apply and appear bumpy and uneven when dry. Paint that has had too much water added will appear streaky and it will be impossible to obtain a flat surface with it. If the right consistency is obtained but the gouache and poster-white have not been mixed thoroughly, this too will cause streaking.

When a new tube of paint is first opened, a clear, thick liquid may come out of the tube before the color. Discard this clear fluid. Do not mix it with the pigment, for it will make the gouache streak.

Next draw some simple geometric shapes on a piece of bristol board. Paint mixed and shapes drawn, you are now ready to begin practicing the flat gouache technique.

With your sable brush, first paint a very thin outline around the inside of your drawn geometric shape (Figure 3.1A). Once the outline is completed you are ready to fill in the remaining area. Gouache tends to dry fast so keep the paint moving as you quickly fill in the shape (Figures 3.1B and 3.1C).

Try not to repaint areas within a shape once the gouache has dried. Repainted areas of a color may appear to be a shade darker than areas painted only once. If you have a complicated shape, paint it in sections. Let paint dry completely to see how flat you have managed to get it. Drying time is only a few minutes. Paint will appear uneven as it is drying.

Once you have had some practice with individual shapes, develop a composition that can be rendered in the flat gouache technique on a 6 × 6-inch square. Mix at least five different colors and paint the entire surface of the square. You may want to practice painting two or three of these small compositions until you feel comfortable with the use of the technique and are ready to employ it in a textile design.

Figure 3.2
DEBI RUBINSTEIN
Summer Drawers (croquis, gouache, 21″ × 19″).
Copyright © 1981, by Debi Rubinstein.

This design was rendered in the flat gouache technique.

A Color Ground

A ground is the background color of the design. A painted ground is one in which the background color has been painted first and motifs or images are then drawn and painted on top. If you work on color paper, this too is considered a color ground, although not painted. Backgrounds may also be blotched.

To paint a ground you will need a wide brush (approximately 1½ inches for an 11 × 14-inch piece of paper). The larger the area of ground that you plan to paint, the larger the brush size you will need.

Mix a large amount of the desired color in a paper or small plastic cup, making sure to mix enough color to cover the area you want to paint. Remember that the paint must be the right consistency—about that of melted ice cream—and colors must be mixed thoroughly to avoid streaking.

Tape each corner of a piece of bristol board to your drawing board or other flat surface. Wet bristol thoroughly and wipe off excess water with a clean rag or paper towel, leaving the surface of the bristol damp.

Now with your wide brush, paint the entire surface rapidly in a horizontal direction. Do not allow the paint to dry in any area. Dip the brush in paint as needed.

Next, quickly repaint the surface in a vertical direction, covering all areas evenly. Once completed, allow to dry. Gouache may appear uneven while drying.

When the painted ground has dried, the paper tends to curl and become uneven. To straighten it, hold the paper at diagonal corners and run the unpainted side back and forth over the edge of the table. Pull paper gently downward while performing this motion. Change and hold at opposite corners, continuing the same process until the

Figure 3.3
Paint a ground by keeping the color moving rapidly over the surface of the paper. Do not allow paint to dry in any area until you have finished.

paper has straightened out (Figure 3.4).

Painted grounds may affect light colors that are painted on top of them. Red, for instance, can bleed through a light color and affect its appearance. For this reason, it is always wise to make small test patches to see how ground colors affect colors painted on top of them.

In a *blotched ground*, motifs are not transferred onto a pre-existing color. Instead, the design is transferred onto white paper (see Chapter 5) and the background color is painted around the motifs. Because the area around a motif is usually complicated, blotching is done in sections using the flat gouache technique. Motifs are first outlined in the blotch color and the flat gouache technique is then followed to paint the entire background, section by section.

Color-paper works well for a ground—if you can find the desired color. There are a variety of commercially printed and dyed color-papers available. Printed color-papers often have a slick surface that the gouache will not adhere to. If you want to paint on these papers, you need to add a drop or two of *Non-Crawl* to the gouache. This clear liquid substance will prevent chipping and help the gouache flow more easily onto these surfaces. When you have finished painting the design, spray it with a workable matte fixative to further prevent chipping and cracking of the gouache.

Painting grounds can save time when doing colorings (see Chapter 7). However the motifs often appear to be more brilliant when set in a blotched ground. Commercially printed or dyed color-papers are also time-saving but the choice of colors is limited. The effect that you are after in your work will determine whether you will use a painted ground, a blotched ground, color-paper or simply use white.

STIPPLING WITH STENCIL

TOOLS AND MATERIALS NEEDED:
BASIC SUPPLIES
AND
STIPPLING SUPPLIES

Stippling is another technique that uses gouache. Stippling is used to obtain textural effects. Stencils are generally used with this technique to define areas where the effect is desired.

Begin by mixing paint in the same manner as described for the flat gouache technique. Here too the consistency of the paint is important. It should be just slightly thicker than that of melted ice cream. Finding the right consistency is, again, often a process of trial and error. It is advisable to practice stippling on some scrap paper without stencils to check the consistency of the paint before beginning.

Cut a simple practice stencil out of bristol board. Use an *X-Acto* knife to do this (Figures 3.5A and 3.5B). To avoid damaging the table or drawing board on which you are cutting, be sure to put a piece of heavier cardboard under the bristol.

The practice stencil can be a simple geometric or organic shape. Be sure to leave ade-

quate space around each stencil hole—approximately three inches on each side. Place stencil on top of white or color-ground paper and hold it in place with two small pieces of masking tape. Cover with scrap paper any ground paper that is exposed beyond the edge of the stencil. This will prevent paint from getting on those areas of the ground where it is not intended.

Hold your toothbrush, bristles up, and apply gouache with mixing brush. Turn bristles of toothbrush downward and, holding a butter knife in your other hand, pull knife across bristles so that paint will spatter onto paper (Figure 3.5C). This can be done in a very rapid motion several times before you will need to apply more paint to the toothbrush. Once you have achieved the desired effect, carefully remove stencil and let dry (Figure 3.5D).

The toothbrush should be held between three and five inches from the surface of the paper. It should be moved slowly back and forth above the area being stippled. The distance the toothbrush is held from the paper and the amount of movement given the brush will affect the results. The longer the paint is stippled in one area, the denser the color will appear. If more stippling is applied to one edge of a shape, the shape will appear to have a more dimensional form.

Try doing several practice shapes. If the same stencil is used several times it may begin to buckle or rise at its edges from the accumulation of paint. The stencil should be held flush with the ground paper. If buckling or rising occurs, weigh stencil down with pennies around its opening.

Once you have established some control with stippling, develop on tracing paper a

**Figure 3.5A and
Figure 3.5B (below)**
Cut a simple practice shape out
of bristol board.

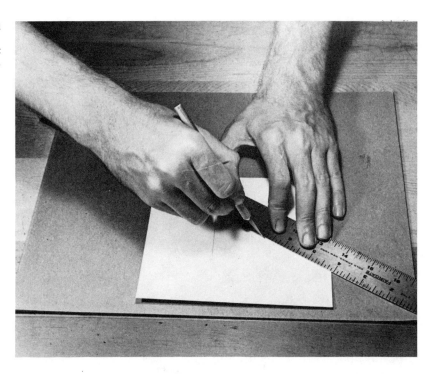

Figure 3.5C
Pull the knife across the bristles of the toothbrush so that the paint will spatter onto the paper.

Figure 3.5D
Carefully remove the stencil and let the stippled shape dry.

25

Figure 3.6
MARCIA JEPSKY
Umbrella Puddles (croquis, gouache, 19¾" × 25½").
Copyright © 1980, Marcia Jepsky.

This design utilizes large areas of stippling. The linear shapes
were resisted with frisket before stippling was applied
through square-shaped stencils. Flat gouache is also used.
Notice the qualities of depth and movement achieved in
this croquis.

small composition that incorporates several
different interlocking or touching shapes.
Rendering interlocking shapes in this manner will take skill and will also help to familiarize you with the process. Use a minimum
of four colors.

Transfer the composition onto a ground
paper, using the tracing and rub-down technique described in Chapter 5. Make stencils

out of bristol board for each shape in your
composition. Do a separate rub-down for
each on individual pieces of bristol. Cut them
in the same manner as you cut the first
practice-stencil.

Place the stencil hole of a shape over the
corresponding shape in the composition you
have transferred onto the ground paper. Stipple, remove the stencil, and let dry. Continue

this process until the entire composition is completed.

When using different colors, use only one color for each stencil hole. It is not advisable to mix stippled colors on top of each other. Doing this tends to tone color down, making it appear dull or dirty. You can achieve a great deal of tonal color change by stippling different areas of a shape for different periods of time.

Your toothbrush will need to be cleaned frequently. Paint dries quickly in bristles and they become less springy, making it difficult to achieve the desired effect. Wet brushes can ruin technique. Water in the brush thins down gouache and makes the stipple effect splotchy and difficult to control. So be sure the brush is completely dry before reusing it. It may be advisable to use several toothbrushes.

Explore the possibilities of making different types of stencils from different materials and in different ways. Tearing shapes out of newsprint can create interesting forms. Frisket can also be used to resist paint from areas of ground paper when using the stippling technique.

Explore the possibilities of the technique and find innovative ways of using it in the development of your textile designs.

RULING PEN AND DRAWING COMPASS

TOOLS AND MATERIALS NEEDED:
BASIC SUPPLIES, RULING PEN, T-SQUARE,
DRAWING BOARD, DRAWING COMPASS

The ruling pen and pen attachment on the drawing compass are two tools that are basically the same. Both are filled with gouache and produce thin, accurate lines. Ink can also be used. Straight lines in stripes and plaids are often the products of the ruling pen. The compass with pen attachment is most commonly used for drawing circles and dots.

It is possible to achieve with these two tools a variety of results much wider than just straight lines and circles. As with any technique or tool, however, it is important to have good technical facility with the more common uses before developing alternative techniques. Practice making some stripes and dots as described below before you become more adventuresome.

RULING PEN

The ruling pen is filled with gouache mixed in the same manner as for the flat gouache technique. The consistency of the paint needed for use in the ruling pen will vary depending on the width of the line you desire. The width of the line is regulated by adjusting the width of the opening between the double blades. Since the paint flows through this opening, thinner lines require thinner paint if paint is to flow evenly.

In general, start by mixing paint to a consistency that is slightly thinner than melted ice cream. Add water, if necessary, to thin out the consistency; but remember to add only a few drops at a time when thinning gouache. Learning the right consistency of paint for the width of line that you need is a

Figure 3.7
Filling the ruling pen.

Figure 3.8
Ruling a straight line.

process of trial and error and can only be discovered through experience in the use of the tool. Paint that is too thick will clog the pen, while paint that is too thin will flow out of the pen too fast and make unwanted blobs. A good rule to follow is that the thinner the line the thinner the consistency of paint required.

The width of the line that the pen will make is adjusted by turning the flat circular knob located just above the pen's point. Ruling pens make only thin-to-very-thin lines. The pen point cannot be opened to too great a width and still function—1/32 of an inch is about the widest. If a thicker line is required, two lines have to be ruled side by side and filled in using the flat gouache technique.

To fill the pen, hold it on its side and put gouache between the two blades of the point with your mixing brush (Figure 3.7). Wipe off excess paint that may accumulate on the outside of the blades with a paper towel. Be sure always to clean and dry the pen thoroughly between each change in paint color and after each use.

Series of parallel lines, such as those used for stripes and plaids, can be obtained through using the ruling pen in conjunction with the drawing board and T-square. Tape a piece of bristol to the drawing board and place the head of the T-square flush with the side of the board. The blade of the T-square should be running horizontally across the board and paper. Lines are ruled by holding pen upright with point next to the T-square (Figure 3.8).

Pull the pen at an even rate across the width of the paper, while holding the tip steady by resting it next to the edge of the T-square. After first stripe is completed, slide the T-square down and into position to start the next stripe. It will be necessary to refill the pen often, usually after every second or third stripe.

The same process can be followed to produce multi-color stripes. If a plaid is desired, simply rule all the stripes in one direction and then turn the paper on its side so that crossing stripes can be ruled at a right angle to those that are already there.

It is advisable to first practice using the ruling pen by doing a plaid or stripe. This will familiarize you with the use of the tool and the technique that you can achieve with it. You can then go on to combine it with other techniques as you develop your design imagery or find new ways to use it in line work. Two examples of work that incorporate the ruling pen line, but in very different ways, are Plate 11 and the design on the cover of this book.

DRAWING COMPASS

Although you may not often have occasion to use the drawing compass, there are times when it is a good tool to know about. The compass has two legs connected by a pivot. One leg has a needle-point end to hold it in place on the paper as it is rotating. The other end has detachable parts: a pen attachment, a needle point, and a lead holder. The width between the legs can be adjusted at the pivot in order to make different-sized circles, dots, and arcs. The compass is held and used as demonstrated in Figure 3.9.

Figure 3.9
The correct way to hold and
use the drawing compass.

In terms of the consistency of gouache and adjustment of line width, the pen attachment for the compass is operated in exactly the same manner as the ruling pen. Fill the pen attachment with gouache and practice circles. If you want to change the circle into a dot, fill the circle in by using the flat gouache technique. Try a composition of circles, dots, and arcs to further your understanding of the use of the compass.

Aligned Dots

Dots that are aligned both vertically and horizontally can easily be produced if you first draw an evenly spaced, squared grid in pencil, to serve as a guide for perfect alignment.

Tape a piece of bristol to the drawing board. Then, using the T-square, draw a horizontal guide line across the top of the paper. Next rest the triangle flush against the T-square and draw a vertical guideline along one side of the paper. These guidelines should be about one inch from the edge of the paper.

Dividers are used to measure an exact distance from each point where a grid line will be drawn (Figure 3.11A). This is done along the guideline. Make the compass into dividers by replacing the pen-point attachment with the needle-point attachment. Adjust the dividers to desired width: the width between needle-points should equal the width between two lines of the grid. The guideline spacing is then measured with the dividers.

Begin at the corner where the vertical

Figure 3.10
TERRY A. GENTILLE
Water Shocks (croquis, gouache, 8¾" × 9").
Copyright © 1980, Terry A. Gentille.

This design was created by using the drawing compass and painting
into the design with gouache.

Figure 3.11A
Dividers are used to measure exact distances between the points where the grid lines will be drawn.

Figure 3.11B
Using the T-square and triangle to draw vertical lines for the squared grid.

Figure 3.12
Aligned dots being drawn with compass. The squared grid serves as a guide for perfect alignment.

and horizontal guidelines cross. Place one point of the divider at this intersection and the other point to fall on the horizontal guideline. Simultaneously make two small holes. Lift the dividers and place one point again into the second hole. At the same time, with the other point, make a third small hole along the horizontal line. Continue doing this along the horizontal and vertical guidelines. Because the width of the dividers remains fixed, the distances between the holes will be equal.

Next, using a T-square and pencil, draw lines horizontally across the paper. The pencil line should start at the center of each hole on the vertical guideline. Next draw the vertical lines, using the triangle resting against the T-square. The pencil line should start at the center of each hole on the horizontal line (Figure 3.11B). You now have a perfectly squared grid.

Place the compass needle-point on each cross point where the horizontal and vertical lines of the grid intersect, and, using the pen attachments, draw a circle (Figure 3.12). Be sure to adjust the width of the compass legs so that the circles will not overlap when drawn. When finished drawing circles, erase the grid and fill in the circles using the flat gouache technique.

FRISKET

TOOLS AND MATERIALS NEEDED:
FRISKET SUPPLIES, BRISTOL BOARD,
MIXING BRUSH

Frisket is a "resist" technique on paper. The frisket is a liquid coating that, when dried, prevents the penetration of color onto the area of the paper where it has been applied. It then resists color that is painted over it. For the frisket technique, either liquid mask frisket or rubber cement may be used and can be applied with a brush or a variety of other tools. However, liquid mask frisket is best for detailed or fine work.

When liquid mask frisket is being applied with a brush, always use an inexpensive mixing brush, never a good sable brush. Frisket dries in brushes easily, ruining their bristles. To guard against damage when using a mixing brush, liquid soap should be rubbed thoroughly into bristles before dipping into frisket. This will allow for easier cleaning and help prevent frisket from drying in bristles. Wash brush immediately after each use.

Liquid mask frisket can also be used in the ruling pen to obtain straight resist lines. In ruling-pen line-resist work, the process is exactly the same as if gouache were being used. Simply fill the pen with liquid mask instead, and proceed according to instructions for the ruling pen given earlier. (Liquid mask frisket is also thinned with water to obtain the right consistency.)

Rubber cement can be used as the frisket if the design work is bolder or looser in its approach to technique. Rubber cement frisket can be applied with a variety of different tools. In fact, just about any object that can be dipped into rubber cement can be used to stamp frisket onto the paper: Nails, pencils, and pieces of bent wire can all be used as tools for this type of application. If cement is too thick it can be thinned with rubber cement thinner.

The following series of photographs illustrates the sequence of steps followed in the creation of a design using paper clips and frisket technique:

To begin, areas of the bristol board are

Figure 3.13A
Liquid frisket being applied
to bristol board with paper clip.

Figure 3.13B
Liquid color being painted
over dried frisket shapes.

blocked out with the liquid mask and allowed
to dry (Figure 3.13A).

A liquid watercolor wash is then painted
over the entire surface of the bristol and this
too is allowed to dry (Figure 3.13B).

The frisket is then peeled or rubbed off
(Figure 3.13C) revealing the white paper

underneath. Thus shapes are created (Figure
3.13D).

Successive coats of frisket and color can
be applied before the final rubbing, creating a
multicolored design. Colors must be applied
from light to dark to obtain maximum contrast.

Practice the technique by developing a

Figure 3.13C
Frisket being rubbed off bristol board
after color has dried.

Figure 3.13D
Finished piece of textured paper.

square (approximately 6 × 6 inches). Use a minimum of three colors (yellow, red, and blue for instance) to create any type of image or surface texture.

Apply frisket to bristol in those areas that are to remain white in the completed practice square, and let dry. Paint yellow

watercolor wash over the entire surface and allow to dry. Do not remove the first application of frisket.

Now apply frisket a second time over those areas of the ground that are to remain yellow. Again let frisket dry and now paint entire surface red.

Figure 3.14
MICHELLE DESVEAUX
Hidden Layers (croquis, frisket with
liquid watercolor, 4¾" × 5½").

36

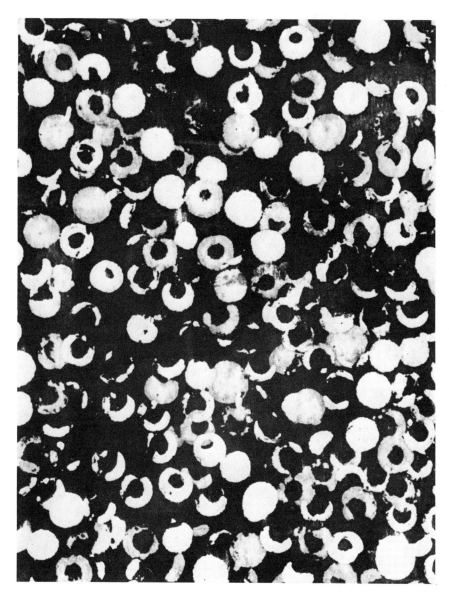

Figure 3.15
GRACE DUNKAS
Untitled (croquis, frisket with
liquid watercolor, 6″ × 8″).
Copyright © 1979, Grace Dunkas.

Finally, once the red watercolor wash has dried, apply frisket for the third time over what is now a red ground. Do not remove first or second application of frisket. This last application of frisket will retain those areas in the square that are to be left red.

Let frisket dry and paint entire surface with watercolor wash of blue. Once the blue has dried, rub or peel off all frisket to reveal a multicolored design image.

A hair dryer can be used to help speed the drying time of liquid watercolor and frisket between applications. Be sure to clean brushes between applications of frisket; otherwise it will dry and destroy brush bristles.

Frisket can be used by itself or mixed

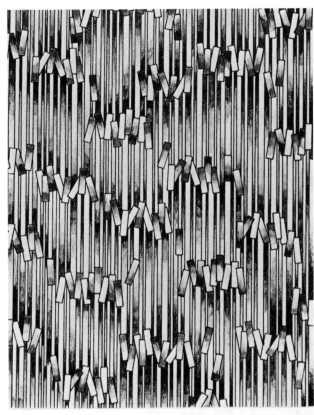

Figure 3.16
TERRY A. GENTILLE
Fluctuation (croquis, pencil, 7⅞″ × 10½″).
Copyright © 1979, Terry A. Gentille.

A croquis using the shaded pencil technique.

Figure 3.17 (below)
GRACE DUNKAS
Sunset Series: I (croquis, pencil and gouache, 18″ × 11¼″).
Copyright © 1980, Grace Dunkas.

An example of an alternative use of pencil technique in a croquis.

with other techniques to develop a variety of interesting design concepts for printed textiles.

SHADED PENCIL

TOOLS AND MATERIALS NEEDED:
COLORED PENCILS AND
PENCIL SHARPENER

Most of us are well aware that texture is inherent in the quality of a pencil line. We have all had years of experience writing with it and the pencil is indeed a familiar tool. But perhaps because it is so familiar, we must be especially careful not to overlook the expressive effects of line and shading that can be achieved through its use.

When the pencil is used as a drawing tool, the texture of the line can be changed from one area to another simply by bearing down harder at some points and exerting less pressure at others. When the pencil is used for shading, it can be made to produce gradations of texture from dark to light within the same shape (see Figure 3.16).

There are two things to remember when using pencil for designing: One, keep the pencil sharp at all times to obtain good technique (electric pencil sharpeners are real time-savers if you do a lot of pencil work). Two, keep each color area clear and distinct. Avoid mixing pencil colors one on top of the other. Pencil colors mixed in this way will not translate into any method of printing except heat transfer.

A quality resembling pencil texture can be obtained in commercial printing through the use of photographic engraving. Once at the engravers, areas of a design are separated by color. Within a single color area in which one pencil color has been used, any type of shading and texture may be achieved. Color areas must be kept clear and distinct to permit the making of color separations. One color can appear directly next to another color but the two should not overlap or be mixed on top of each other. This is the only limitation in using pencil for designing of printed textiles.

To begin, make several different types of line and shaded areas of a single gradated color. Once you have found different qualities in the use of the pencil, create a small composition, keeping in mind that colors should not overlap one another. When you have practiced the technique, it can be used by itself or with other techniques in the development of a croquis.

FLUSH-JOINING

TOOLS AND MATERIALS NEEDED:
FLUSH-JOINING SUPPLIES,
ONE OR MORE SURFACE TEXTURES

Flush-joining is a method of inlaying one piece of paper into another so that the finished surface is flush. It can be used as a designing technique to create an effect somewhat like collage. In certain instances it is used simply to attach two identical pieces of paper to make a larger designing surface. It may also be used to correct a mistake in a design by inlaying a new piece of ground paper over the error.

As a designing technique, it is primarily used when papers that have textural effects created by marbleizing, surface rubbings, or frisket textures are inlaid into ground papers. Whatever your purpose, in each instance the weight of the paper used for the texture and the weight of the ground paper should be similar.

Figure 3.18
MARCIA JEPSKY
Crumpled Textures (croquis, crayon and watercolor, 25½″ × 29″).
Copyright © 1981, Marcia Jepsky.

A design created through the use of surface rubbings.

Surface Textures

Marbleizing An interesting surface texture can be created by floating oil-based enamel paint on water and then transferring the paint onto a piece of paper. This is done by gently setting the piece of paper on top of the floating paint for a second or two and then lifting it off. The paint will transfer and create a swirling textured surface.

Fill an aluminum roasting pan—the disposable type found in supermarkets—or other disposable container with plain water. You will need to thin the enamel with turpentine to achieve the right consistency for floating. Paint that is too thick will sink to the bottom of the pan. It is possible to float several colors of paint simultaneously to achieve a multicolored effect. To obtain some control over the marbleizing pattern, you can push the color around on the surface of the water with a pencil or stick.

Surface Rubbings Rubbings are made by placing a piece of paper over a textured relief surface, such as a brick wall, metal screening, broom bristles, or a wooden floor. The paper is then rubbed with color pencil, pastels or crayons so that the relief surface underneath makes a colored impression on the paper.

Frisket Textures These are made according to the frisket technique described earlier. Try applying frisket with a sponge or wadded-up paper towels to obtain different types of textural effects.

Flush-Joining Technique

Begin with a textured surface paper—henceforth referred to as "T-paper"—and a ground paper—henceforth referred to as "G-paper." The object is to inlay the T-paper into the G-paper and retain a flush surface.

Practice this technique by inlaying a simple triangular shape of T-paper into the G-paper. First draw the shape of the triangle in pencil on the T-paper (Figure 3.19A).

Attach the T-paper, textured side up, to the G-paper with masking tape to prevent slipping during cutting. (The masking tape is temporary and will be removed when the flush is completed.)

Place the joined papers on a heavy cardboard cutting surface and, with an *X-Acto* knife, cut through both T-paper and G-paper. Cut only two sides of the triangle (Figure 3.19B). You will probably need to use a metal ruler to guide the cutting of the straight lines.

Turn the G-paper over; the T-paper remains attached with masking tape. There should be a "V" shape cut through to the

back of the G-paper which corresponds to the two triangular sides just cut.

Lift the "V" shape on the back-side of the G-paper to reveal the back-side section of the T-paper that appears through the cuts. With clear tape, secure the back-side section of the T-paper, which is showing through the cut, to the back-side of the G-paper (Figure 3.19C). This will prevent the T- and G-papers from slipping when making the final cut.

Turn the G-paper over and cut the final side of the triangle, as before. Be sure to cut all the way through the T- and G-papers.

Turn the G-paper over again and discard the triangular piece of G-paper. The triangular shaped back-side of the T-paper should be taped completely to the back-side of the G-paper and lightly burnished.

Turn the G-paper over and remove the masking tape and the rest of the T-paper that is not part of the triangle (Figure 3.19D). The result is a triangular shape of the textured surface paper inlaid into the ground paper (Figure 3.19E).

Flush-joining can also be used with very complicated and intricate shapes. It is important to remember that, to avoid slipping of papers while cutting is in progress, the back-sides of the two papers must be secured often. If either paper slips, small holes will appear between the T- and G-papers. A good rule to follow is that the more complicated the shape, the more often the back-sides should be taped during cutting.

Once you understand this technique, it can be incorporated into a croquis. So we should consider next how to match a specific area of the T-paper to a desired location in the croquis layout and flush-join it to the ground paper. To do this, the preliminary layout must be completed on tracing paper

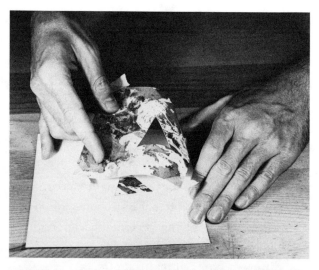

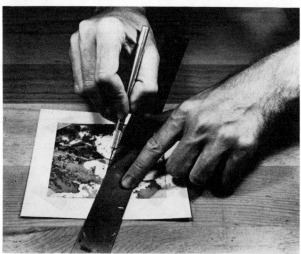

Figure 3.19A (top left)
A ground paper and textured paper for flush-joining. Notice the triangular shape drawn on the textured paper.

Figure 3.19B (middle left)
Cutting simultaneously through the textured paper and ground paper.

Figure 3.19C (left)
Taping the back-side of the textured paper to the back-side of the ground paper through the V cut.

Figure 3.19D (top right)
The excess textured paper is removed.

Figure 3.19E (above right)
The result: a textured, triangular shape, inlaid into the ground paper.

and then transferred to the ground paper (see "Tracings and Rub-Downs," page 57).

Once the transfer has been completed, do not remove the tracing paper. Instead, remove only the tape on the bottom two corners of the tracing-paper layout, leaving the top two corners taped to the ground paper. You then lift the tracing paper and slip the T-paper between the tracing and the G-paper. The T-paper, which can be seen through the tracing paper, can be shifted about so that a specific area will fall directly at the desired location in the layout.

Once you have positioned the T-paper, lift the tracing and tape the G-paper with masking tape. Flip the tracing over the T- and G-papers again and rub-down onto the T-paper the shape or area of the layout that you want to flush onto the G-paper. The rub-down on the T-paper will serve as your cutting guideline, and the two papers are now ready to be flush-joined.

Figure 3.20
MARCIA JEPSKY
Rain (croquis, *Xerox*-duplicated rubbings, 25″ × 42″).
Copyright © 1981, Marcia Jepsky.

This croquis makes inventive use of the flush-joining technique and rubbings.

Many individuals become quite lost when confronted with the task of finding "inspiration." But inspiration can come from any stimulus that evokes the creative process. Sources of inspiration are literally everywhere. But more importantly, it is the designer's artistic sensibility and interpretive style that brings creative design into being.

Ultimately creativity develops through continual awareness and hard work combined with the curiosity to seek and explore new sources of artistic stimulation and modes of expression. Following are some new and traditional sources to explore.

CHAPTER FOUR

Design inspiration

TRADITIONAL SOURCES

In textile print design there are many traditional sources of inspiration. Designs called *figuratives* are based on the forms of animals, birds, insects, sea life, and the human body.

Conversationals is a category which encompasses various objects such as playing cards, bicycles, umbrellas, and fans. *Scenics,* consisting of outdoor settings and landscapes, and *florals,* based on plant life, have long been used as reference sources. Other sources of inspiration include a whole range of *geometric*

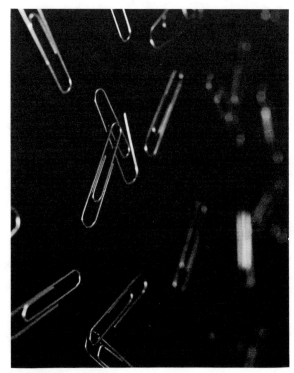

Figure 4.1A (right)
The source of inspiration.

Figure 4.1B (below)
GRACE DUNKAS
Flying Paper Clips
(croquis, pencil, 12″ × 13″).
Copyright © 1979, Grace Dunkas.

The croquis of the design inspired by
the source.

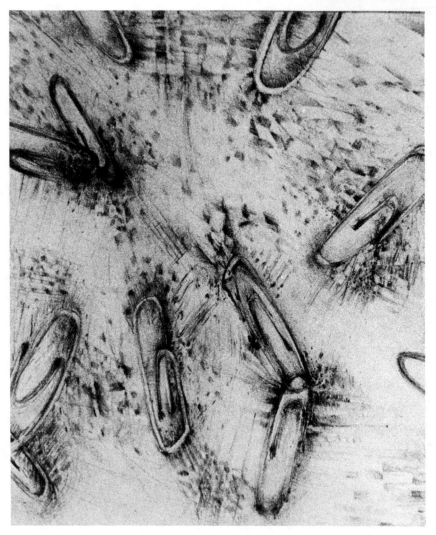

forms and *textured surfaces* such as animal skins and marble. The long established relationships between these images and printed textiles would make it seem difficult—if not impossible—to do anything new or innovative with them. But this is not the case.

Many factors may influence the way a particular designer will interpret traditional reference sources. Technology—the development of new processes in printing and engraving—can be one influence. There are so many methods by which textiles are printed today that practically any design, regardless of its complexity, can be printed by one method or another. Contemporary trends can influence artistic direction to a great extent. The designer may respond either by designing in accordance with trends or by reacting against them. But perhaps the most important element in the innovative interpretation of any of the traditional reference sources is the designer's own individual style. This personalized interpretation, often referred to as the *hand,* develops in each designer over time, through training, observation, and practice with aesthetic and technical elements. Although it is possible for very experienced designers to work in more than one hand, the hand is somewhat like a signature—no two are exactly alike.

NEW SOURCES

Virtually any object has the potential for development into a textile image. The most common objects—things we see in our daily routine—are possible design sources. Take inspiration from a cracked egg shell or some scattered paper clips. Even the television set can be a source of inspiration for the development of a motif. Images can be derived from trash in the streets or from practically any natural phenomenon—from the beautiful patterning of waves on the sea to qualities of rain or lightning. Architectural structures and cloud formations can be used separately or in conjunction with each other. Our environment is filled with a multitude of visual references waiting to be developed into designs. Through awareness you will discover endless sources of inspiration.

Moreover, the designing of a motif is not always motivated by a reference source. The catalyst for new ideas is sometimes the discovery of a new medium, technique, or tool. The designer may create a whole range of interesting concepts based on the use of these alone. Once you have control of a new medium or can reproduce a technique with fair consistency, it becomes part of your working vocabulary. But professional designers search constantly for new ways of developing images and making marks.

Another approach to sources of inspiration is called *concept designing,* in which the designer attempts to convey a feeling, a mood, or a concept, such as "stillness," "activity," "density," or "indifference." Concepts such as "light in space" or "line evolution" make for interesting fabric designs because the interpretations can be done on a very personal level.

The biggest obstacles to creativity for most students to overcome usually involve their own preconceived notions of what a textile design is or should be. Inspiration can come from virtually any source. There is no

Figure 4.2
SUSAN GLASSER
Kitchen Series (croquis, gouache,
20½″ × 19½″).
Virtually any object has the potential for
development into a textile image.

need to limit yourself to an established approach to designing. Rather, you should avail yourself of a variety of creative avenues. There is no one solution to any design problem.

The development of a textile design often takes place in four basic steps. As a beginning designer you will want to follow this procedure:

1. Selection of one or more reference sources.
2. Choice of one or more techniques and media.
3. Development of a new image (motif) or images based upon an interpretation of the reference source and using a suitable technique.
4. Use of one or more images in a layout or compositional arrangement appropriate to the textile print format (croquis).

The initial learning period is one of discovery and excitement. It is important to realize, however, that expertise is not attained over-

night. Just as the technique for each step is mastered in stages, artistic development is an ongoing process which continues throughout the designer's creative life.

KEEPING NOTES

Once you have begun the search for references you will be confronted with countless ideas, images and colors—more than you can possibly remember. For this reason it is worth keeping a "Design Inspiration Sketch Book." Here you should keep sketches and ideas that might be used in developing a design. Drawing is very important. Keeping records of what you see by drawing will help develop your visual sensitivity and cultivate your imagination. You might also want to collect photographs, swatches of color, dried leaves, or anything else that inspires you.

EXPOSURE AND AWARENESS

For most beginning designers, the greatest sources of stimulation for creative growth and development are provided by exposure and awareness. Visiting current exhibitions in museums and galleries provides exposure to the creative works of others. Reading books stimulates and enriches the mind and imagination. Travel, when possible, and the experience of different ways of life and cultures, can be extraordinarily enriching for an artist. Museums should also be visited for historic and ethnic references. Much can be gained by studying the design elements of different cultures and periods. Although you would not wish to copy a cultural style or historic period—this kind of work falls into the category of textile reproduction—you would likely be inspired to synthesize what you see into new creations of your own.

Visual awareness is another important concern. Be aware of your surroundings; notice every detail and more. Ask yourself "How and what do I see?" Define this response and record your answers in your sketch book. Then look and ask again. Continue to do this until you have exhausted all the possibilities; then begin the process again.

It is interesting to note that different persons looking at the same object often have varying interpretations of what they see. Even when it is seen from the same angle, in the same light, and at the same time, the way an object looks can depend upon the visual awareness of each individual.

Try this exercise to help expand your own visual awareness. Choose an object small enough to carry around to various places out of its usual context—a hard boiled egg, for example. Set one in your room or in the sand at the beach. How does the environmental space around the egg change its appearance from one setting to another? View the egg from a distance of an inch. What is the relationship between the egg and the space? Notice the egg at different times of day and in different light settings. How does it change in terms of color, form or mood? What is the relationship between the egg and its shadow at these times? This is a simple exercise in viewing and awareness, but one that can be highly enlightening.

Lastly, be aware of the process of designing. Images and layouts can change and develop from the initial idea. Often a beginning designer is so strongly focused on the idea of the finished design that many exciting possibilities that could develop during its execution are overlooked. There are times when "mistakes" are more exciting than the original intention. Allow yourself room to grow. Be flexible and open to experimentation.

Figure 4.3
Design inspiration is everywhere. Here is one of nature's reference sources in a ready-made croquis format.

Before being developed into repeat, most textile designs are conceived in the form of a sketch. This sketch, which may be drawn, or painted, or both, is called a *croquis* (**crow-key**). The croquis must contain all of the design elements to be printed on the cloth, including complete motifs and their compo-sitional layout, color, scale, and technique to be used.

Of critical importance for the designer is the understanding of the special composi-tional requirements of the croquis, which are totally different from those of painting and drawing. Unlike the picture-images of a paint-

CHAPTER FIVE

The croquis

ing or drawing, which are arranged in relationship to the edges of a canvas or piece of paper, the design elements of a croquis are arranged in relationship to each other. The boundaries created by the edges of the paper are irrelevant to the composition; the croquis must indicate the way the pattern will look when extended beyond the four edges of the paper and printed on unlimited lengths of cloth.

The design intention for every element in the croquis must be explicit. Remember that you are not designing just for yourself; textile designs are bought and used by an

Figure 5.1A
Pushpins.

Figure 5.1B
Geranium leaves.

Although these photographs are of
actual objects, both meet the
compositional requirements of the
croquis.

industry. If the manufacturer cannot understand your intention for the repetition of the
pattern or if there is inconsistency in the way
a technique is used, your sketch may be considered unfinished—or useless.

Once you have developed the images or
motifs for your croquis, the next step is to do
a layout on tracing paper. This layout will
later be transferred onto the ground paper—
the paper on which the design is actually
painted. Two principal considerations of the
croquis layout are direction and density.

Figure 5.2
NANCY FEDOROWICZ
Birds (croquis, gouache, 14″ × 18″).
Copyright © 1979, Nancy Fedorowicz.

This croquis provides a good example of a one-directional layout.

Direction

Layout direction refers to the positions of the motifs and is especially important when the motifs have definite tops and bottoms. In a one-directional layout, the motifs would all face the same way. In an animal pattern, for example, all the heads would face upright in the same direction.

In a two-directional pattern, the animals' heads would be placed both upright and upside down so that the length of cloth could be turned completely around and still look the same. This is especially useful for cutting to avoid wastage of fabric.

Most thrifty of all is the multi-directional pattern, which looks correct from all sides. Here the heads of the animals could be turned in any direction. Fabrics for furnishings tend to be one-directional; apparel fabrics are more usually two-directional or multi-directional.

Density

The next consideration for the layout is the density of recurring motifs within the compositional arrangement. Motifs may be arranged so that they are densely placed or even touching. At the other extreme, there may be a great deal of space around each motif so that large amounts of ground are showing. Both approaches are correct and anything in between is possible. There may also be areas of densely spaced motifs and areas of sparsely placed motifs within the same design. This is appropriate, providing

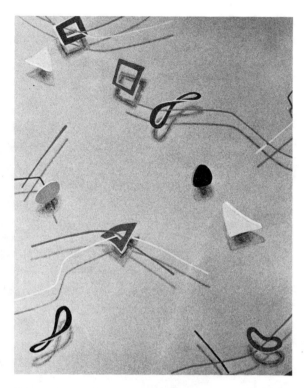

Figure 5.3
TERRY A. GENTILLE
Suspended Geometrics (croquis, gouache and pencil, 16⅜" × 18½").
Copyright © 1979, Terry A. Gentille.

This croquis has a one-directional layout. Notice the difference in density of motifs from Figures 0.1, 1.2, and 5.2.

the finished croquis is large enough to show entire areas recurring in compositional relationship to each other.

In the past, when developing the layout, various systems of underlying straight or curvilinear grid structures, called *ovigals*, were employed to aid the designer in the surface arrangement and break up. But because so many of today's creative designers strive to create designs that have "never been seen before" these structures are used less frequently than they once were. They, neverthe-

Figure 5.4

NANCY FEDOROWICZ
Branches (croquis, gouache, 11″ × 11″).

This croquis provides an example of a two-directional layout.
Turn the design upside down and note that it still appears "correct."

Figure 5.5 (left)
ELEANOR R. COWEN
Dash (croquis, oil pastel, 29¾″ × 30″).
Copyright © 1980, Eleanor R. Cowen.

Because of its horizontal emphasis, this layout is two-directional. Other examples of two-directional layout are Figures 1.1 and 3.16.

Figure 5.6
SUSAN GLASSER
Boxes (croquis, gouache, 19½″ × 17″).
Copyright © 1980, Susan Glasser.

This croquis provides an example of a multi-directional layout. Turn the design and view it from any angle—it always looks "correct." Other examples of multi-directional layouts are Figures 3.2, 3.6, and 3.18.

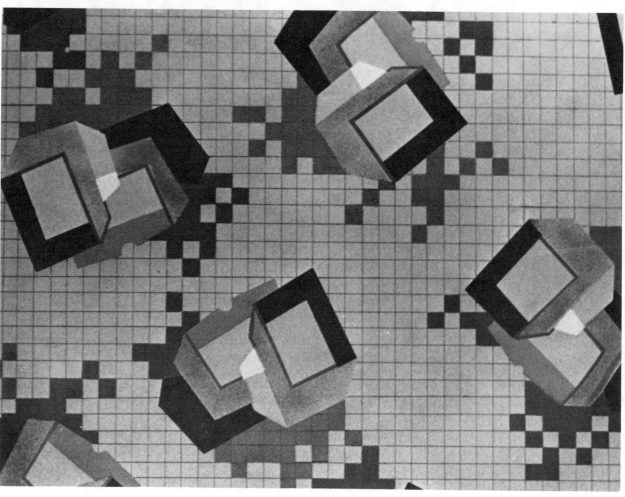

less, remain as possibilities for use in composing layouts.

DEVELOPING THE LAYOUT

Draw a square or rectangle on a piece of tracing paper, leaving ample space around it. These defined boundaries are only a tentative guideline; they can be enlarged or reduced depending on the needs of the composition as it is developed. The size of the square or rectangle is determined by the size of motifs and compositional arrangement in the layout.

Next, on small pieces of tracing paper, trace outlines of all the motifs that you plan to incorporate in the design. Now begin to develop the composition within the squared area according to the decisions you have made regarding the layout direction and the density of your motifs. This is done by arranging the smaller traced motifs under the larger squared area and retracing them onto the larger sheet.

You may find that it will take a lot of shifting and changing before you arrive at a satisfactory composition. Lightly trace motifs so they can easily be erased and shifted if necessary. Spend time on the development of your layout; a good layout usually takes time. Don't be inhibited about beginning again. Tracing paper is inexpensive and you may need to use several sheets before you have finished.

Remember that in developing your layout, the composition must indicate the way the pattern will look when it is extended beyond the edge of the page. Motifs and groups of motifs or other design elements used in the layout must appear more than once within the squared area. Study the variety of examples of croquis in this book so that you can get a better visual understanding of this.

TRACINGS AND RUB-DOWNS

Once you have completed your layout, you are ready to do a backing. Because the layout is done on tracing paper, it can be turned over and seen in reverse from the back-side. The backing is a tracing of the layout in reverse, and is made so that the layout can be transferred to the final piece of ground paper.

To do the backing, you will need another sheet of tracing paper, slightly larger than the layout sheet. Tape this sheet to the layout at each corner. On the backing sheet, trace the layout in reverse with a 2B pencil; be sure to trace the boundary lines. When you have finished, lift one corner to check that all motifs have been traced. Then separate the two sheets and label each.

You are now ready to transfer your backing by burnishing, or rubbing it down, onto the final ground paper. This is done by taping the backing to the ground paper at each corner, traced-leaded side against the ground paper. Holding a metal teaspoon by its handle, rub over the traced area with the edge of the spoon. This will transfer the motifs onto the ground paper.

Figure 5.7
A backing that has been burnished onto ground paper.
One corner is lifted, revealing the reverse image on the
tracing paper.

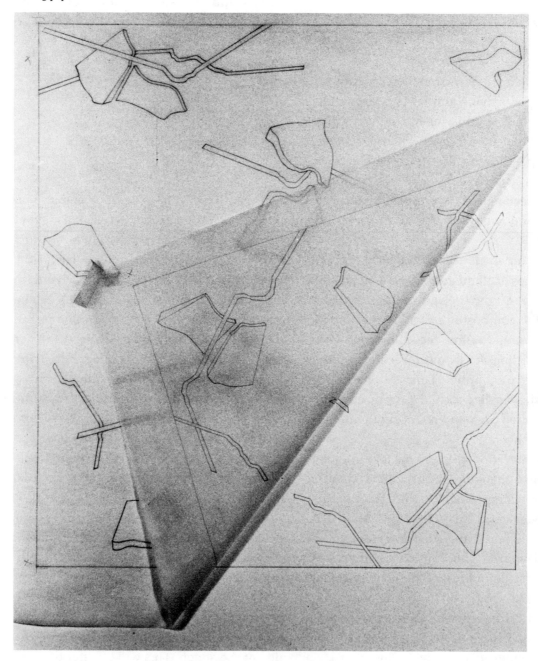

After you have rubbed all areas, lift one corner to check that all motifs have transferred completely. Remove the backing. The finished layout is now transferred to the ground paper and ready to be rendered in whatever technique you have chosen.

Rub-down options may be necessary if you want to transfer the layout onto a painted gouache ground. The layout backing cannot be burnished on a painted ground because the gouache will become shiny and slightly changed in color. To avoid this, use the same transfer process, but instead of burnishing, each motif must be carefully retraced, line by line, so that the graphite tracing on the reverse side of the tracing paper will transfer onto the final painted page.

If the layout backing is to be transferred onto a dark ground, the graphite pencil will not show. It is possible to do the backing in white pencil. Be sure to keep the pencil sharp at all times. The layout backing can then be transferred with the same line-tracing process used for the transfer of a backing onto a painted ground.

TROUBLE-SHOOTING

Incomplete composition of the croquis is a common error made by beginning designers. One reason for this is that the designer, although aware of the design intention, simply does not make the croquis large enough to show how the pattern's design elements or areas of motifs recur in relationship to each other. If the composition is incomplete it cannot be considered correct.

Inconsistency of image and technique are other common problems. A variety of intentional differences can appear within a design in a recurring fashion. Inconsistency of image involves motifs within the croquis which are meant to look similar or identical, but appear slightly different. This is usually the result of careless rendering or painting.

Consistency of technique is of critical concern if your croquis is to be considered correct for the printed textile format. Any way of making a mark, drawing a line, or using a texture is correct if you can duplicate and use it in a consistent manner throughout the design. Inconsistency usually occurs simply because the designer lacks experience in using a particular technique. The best way to avoid inconsistency in the croquis is to experiment with a technique, determining the way you want to use it, before it goes into the finished work.

The croquis is not a repeat. Many beginning designers try to develop the croquis by putting motifs into a repeat system. This severely limits the compositional possibilities of the croquis. Note the distinctions between recurring motifs and design elements, as described in this chapter, and the croquis developed into repeat, as described in the next chapter.

Remember that every element in the croquis must represent an explicit design intention. Anything vague or inconsistent can only be considered a mistake.

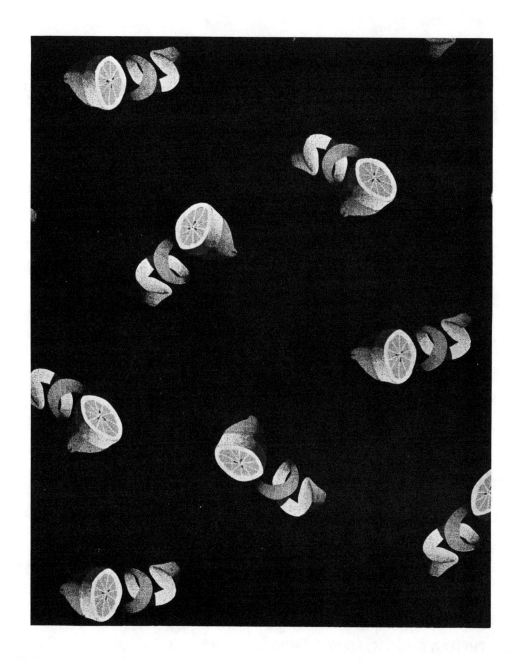

The concept of repeat is one of the most critical for the textile designer to understand, for the repeat is the prerequisite of production printing that makes possible unlimited amounts of patterned surface to be printed from one small sketch. Working within the technical framework of the repeat challenges the abilities of the creative designer.

As you have seen, the croquis represents all of the design elements to be printed on the cloth. The repeat is the organization of the design elements of the croquis into units that recur at constant intervals, according to a system.

Before you can deal effectively with different repeat systems and techniques, you

CHAPTER SIX

Repeat

must understand the function of each component of the repeat: the unit, the system, and the layout, or engraving sketch.

THE UNIT

The unit represents all elements of the croquis organized into predetermined measure-

ments of length and width so that when identical units are placed next to each other, they will form a continuous pattern. The vertical repeat of the unit along the printed surface is called the *length repeat*; the horizontal repeat of the unit across the cloth is called the *side repeat*.

The unit-length measurement is determined by the type of printing method used. In rotary printing, it corresponds to the circumference of the copper roller or rotary screen. In flat-bed screen printing, it is equal to the length of the screen. The unit length runs on the straight grain of the cloth, parallel to the selvage.

The unit-width measurement is determined by the sizes of motifs and by the layout. It may be as small as two inches or it may run across the cloth's entire width. The unit width runs on the cross grain of the cloth, from selvage to selvage.

The Repeated Motif

A motif is simply one element of the design. Within each unit, there may be a number of different motifs, or all motifs can be the same.

When the identical units are repeated systematically over the printed surface, all motifs in the unit are also systematically repeated. A motif appearing in the same position in each adjoining unit is called a *repeated motif.*

THE SYSTEM

There are two systems by which the units of a design can be repeated: the aligned system and the offset system. Using one system or the other, virtually any design can be put into repeat.

THE ALIGNED SYSTEM

In the aligned system, the units are positioned so that they align both vertically and hori-

Figure 6.1
An engraving sketch in aligned repeat: unit length 15″, unit width 15½″, prepared for flat-bed screen printing (gouache).
Courtesy of Grace Dunkas, Copyright © 1981.

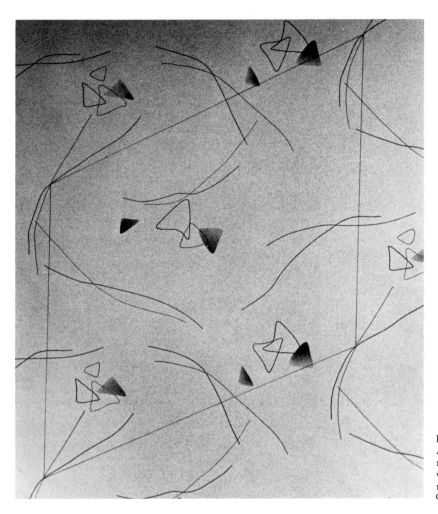

zontally. This means that if you draw straight lines from center to center of repeated motifs, the result will be a squared or rectangular grid. In Figure 6.1, for example, the straight lines, which are intersecting the motifs at similar points, create a square.

THE OFFSET SYSTEM

In the offset system, the interlocking units are positioned so that they align vertically. But each successive length of units is offset on the side repeat so that the horizontal alignment is shifted. This means that, for example, if the unit length on a piece of printed fabric is eighteen inches, and the side repeat is offset

4½ inches, it will take four adjoining units repeating on the side before the units are again positioned on the same level. If straight lines are drawn from center to center of repeated motifs, the effect will be that of rows of parallelograms, each adjoining row aligned vertically and offset horizontally. You can see the parallelogram produced in Figure 6.2, which shows an offset unit repeat.

The offset can occur at any point on the length edge of the unit. Its length can be in whole inches or fractions of an inch. Traditionally the offset is known as a "drop," the most common drop occurring halfway down the unit-length measurement.

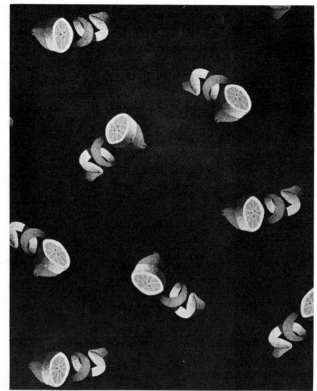

Figure 6.3 (right)
HARRIET SAWYER
Lemon Peel
Copyright © 1981, Harriet Sawyer for New Wave Fabrics, Ltd.

Offset repeat: unit length 25″, unit width 15″, discharge printed with rotary screens, four screens, 45″ width.
In this design, the repeat motif is in the upper and lower left corners and at center right.

Figure 6.4 (below)
Honahlee
Copyright © 1975, Groundworks Inc. Fabric courtesy of Patricia Green.

Offset repeat: unit length 15″, unit width 23½″, hand screen printed, four screens, 49″ width.
In this design, the repeat motif is in the upper and lower left corners and at center right.

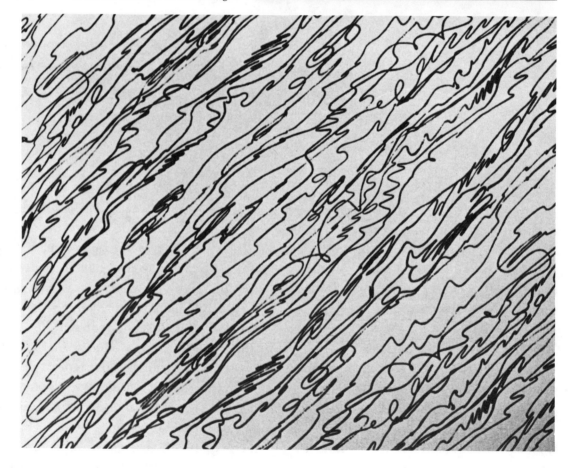

THE ENGRAVING SKETCH

The engraving sketch is the croquis developed into repeat. It is so called because it is the sketch from which the engravers work to engrave the design onto the rollers or screens. The engraving sketch is a facsimile on paper of the way the design will look when extended over yards of cloth. The sketch consists of a series of identical, interlocking units, repeated according to a system. It must contain at least one complete repeat unit with enough information from adjoining units to clearly indicate the effect that will be created by the design in repeat.

The preliminary work of composing the croquis into repeating units is first done in outline on tracing paper. This *repeat layout,* once completed, is transferred to the ground paper (see "Tracings and Rub-Downs," page 57). Or, as the photographs on this page illustrate, you can also work directly on the ground paper (Figures 6.5A–6.5E).

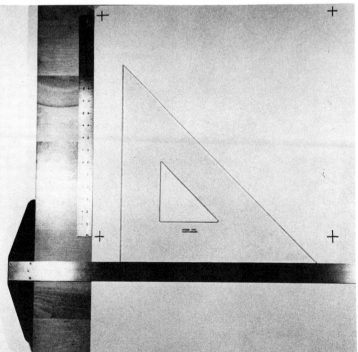

STEP BY STEP REPEAT

Figure 6.5A (above right)
To put a croquis into repeat, begin by tracing the design onto tracing paper. Then make a backing.

Figure 6.5B (right)
The repeat layout must be squared. Use the T-square and triangle to make register makes (+) in pencil on the ground paper. The register marks approximate the area of the repeat unit. In this repeat layout, the unit length is eighteen inches. (This engraving sketch is prepared for roller printing.)

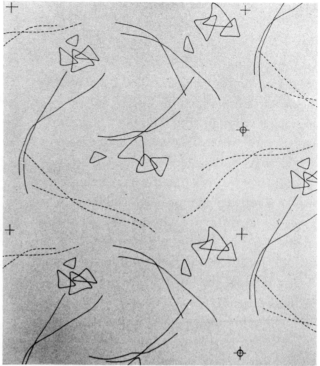

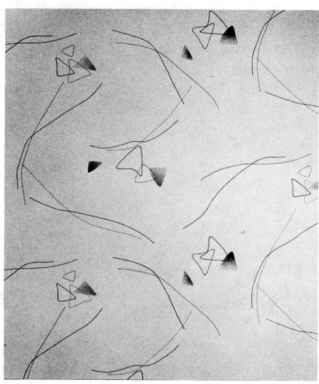

Figure 6.5C (above left)
Use the traced backing to transfer the main motifs of the design into the areas defined by the register marks on the length repeat. Take care to match the corner marks on the traced backing to the register marks.
The side repeat is determined next; in this layout the offset repeat system is used. The register marks (+) indicating the side repeat are drawn in pencil. The corner marks on the traced backing are matched to the side repeat register marks. The same motifs that were transferred onto the length repeat are rubbed down in the side repeat positions.

Figure 6.5D (above right)
More motifs are added to fill in the gap in the layout (indicated in the photograph by broken lines). Notice that although these motifs are positioned differently from the motifs in the original croquis, the visual appearance of the repeat layout remains the same as that of the croquis layout.

Figure 6.5E (right)
The repeat layout is rendered in gouache, using the ruling pen and stippling. The register marks are erased and the finished engraving sketch is ready to be sent to the mill.

STRIPING

The layout must be thoroughly checked for striping, an unwanted element in the design that becomes evident which the unit is put into repeat. For example, a repetition of color can unintentionally create unwanted color stripes. Crowded or uneven distribution of compositional elements can also create unwanted bands across the cloth, as can motifs which, because of size or color, become noticeable at regular intervals. A good way to check for striping is to have photostats made of the repeat layout before it is painted, and paste them together into a larger repeating area.

When developing a croquis into a repeating unit, it may be necessary to make changes in some elements of the design. For example, it is possible that rearrangement of the composition will be necessary to fit into the unit-length measurement. There are also instances when an adaptation of a motif is required. In either case the finished design in repeat, although altered, should give the same visual impression as the original croquis from which it was taken.

MOTIF ADAPTATION

The following example of motif adaptation will illustrate its application. A croquis was being developed into a repeat with an eighteen-inch unit-length measurement, according to the aligned repeat system. It consisted of palm branches tossed in different directions and touching each other at their edges. The

effect was a continuous pattern of palm branches with no spacing between them.

Each branch occupied about a four-inch square. Four complete branches covered sixteen inches of the eighteen-inch unit-length. A blank space or gap of two inches was left. This space was too small for another whole branch, and adding partial brances was not acceptable. The problem was how to fill the gap and maintain the continuity of equally sized, touching branches over the entire surface.

The solution to the problem was an adaptation of the palm branch. The artist did this by adding two extra leaves to each branch, enlarging the branch size to 4½ inches. This measurement multiplied by four was equal to the eighteen-inch unit-length measurement required for the repeat. The appearance of the design, when put into repeat, remained visually the same, even though the branches were slightly enlarged—and the problem of discontinuity created by the two-inch gap was solved.

BORDER PRINTS AND
DRAPERY FABRICS

Border prints and drapery fabrics need special care in the design of the repeat layout. A border print is designed to run along one edge or across the entire width of the cloth. As the name suggests, it is designed to be cut into patterns—such as those for skirts and dresses—that have printed borders. The design of the layout must take this into consideration and leave enough space on one edge of the cloth so that a hem can be turned

Figure 6.6
HARRIET SAWYER
Neon Highway
Copyright © 1979, Harriet Sawyer for New Wave Fabrics, Ltd.

Border print: repeat length 25″, discharge printed with rotary
screens, seven screens, 45″ width.

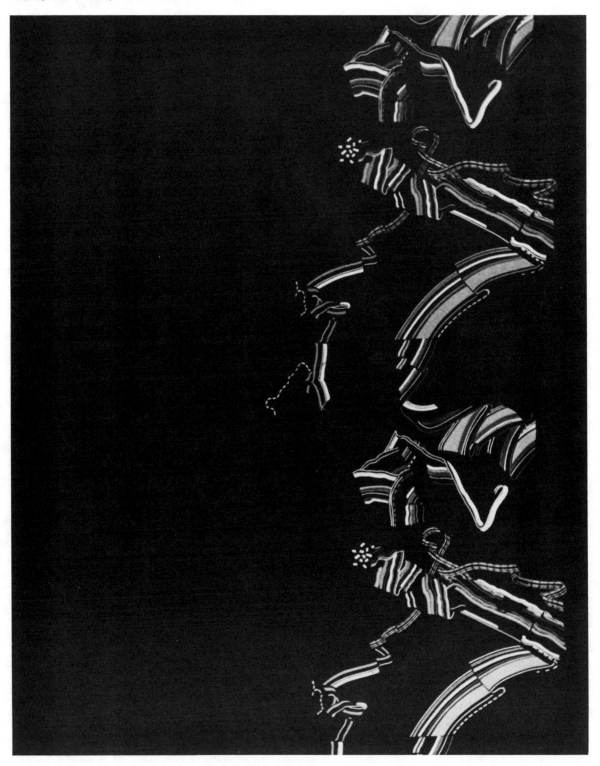

under without interfering with the pattern. A space of two to 2½ inches is generally adequate (Figure 6.6).

A drapery fabric is designed so that the sides of the cloth can be matched edge to edge, maintaining a continuous flow of design elements when lengths are sewn together. This can be done by designing the repeat layout for the full width of the cloth (minus selvage allowance), or by using a unit-width measurement that divides equally into the width of the fabric minus selvage allowance. In either case, images at the edge of the fabric are printed in half so that when the cloth is seamed together they are matched to form a completed motif (Figure 6.7).

Figure 6.7
FEDE CHETI
Penne di struzzo
An original Fede Cheti design, produced and styled by Groundworks, Inc., Copyright © 1981. Fabric courtesy of Patricia Green.

Aligned repeat matching at selvage: unit length 35″, unit width 52″, automatic flat-bed printed, eleven screens, 52″ width.

The half ribbon motifs on the right selvage are matched to the half ribbon motifs on the left selvage so that when the fabric is seamed together, the ribbons form one complete motif.

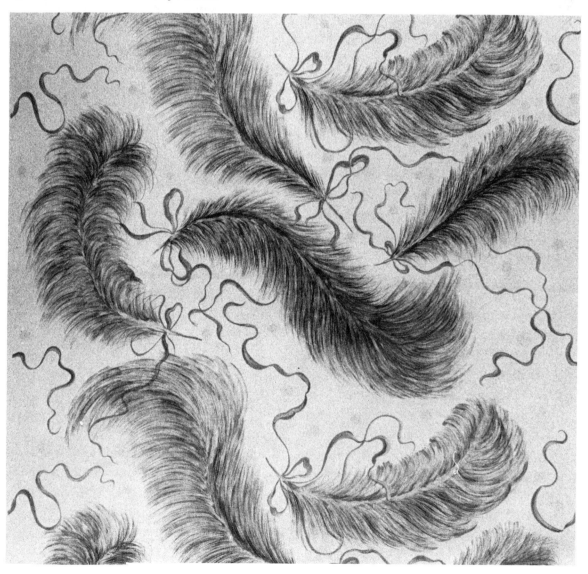

REPEAT SIZES

The repeat size refers to the unit-length measurement. The unit-length measurement is either equal to or a divisor of the circumference of the roller, rotary screen, or heat transfer cylinder, or to the screen length.

Most designs are sold in the croquis format before they are put into repeat because repeat sizes may vary from one manufacturer to another, depending on printing methods. The designer develops the croquis with knowledge of approximate repeat sizes that can be used. Once sold, the croquis is then put into actual repeat according to the manufacturer's size specifications. The exact repeat size, the width of the cloth, and the type of printing and engraving method to be used, are known by the designer prior to painting the engraving sketch.

You will need a lot of practice with doing repeats to familiarize yourself with the process. Select a repeat size and work within its framework. The printing techniques commonly used in the industry require repeat sizes as listed below (see also Chapter 8, "Industrial Printing Processes"):

Roller printing The circumference of an engraved roller can be from fifteen to eighteen inches. The repeat unit-length can equal the roller circumference measurement or it can be a divisor of it: for example, if a roller has a sixteen-inch circumference, a unit with an eight-inch length can be used twice to equal the roller circumference measurement. A unit with a 5⅓-inch length can be used, repeating three times to equal the sixteen-inch circumference. Or a unit with a four-inch length can be used four times.

Hand screen printing This process makes possible very long unit-lengths without limiting the number of screens. Fabrics have been hand screened that have unit lengths as long as seventy-two inches.

Automatic flat-bed printing Long unit-lengths are made possible in this process. The length of the unit can vary depending on the type of printing equipment and the number of colors desired. A length of approximately fifty-three inches can use as many as twenty colors. Large lengths of 120 inches can use up to five colors and even larger lengths of 200 inches are limited to one color. (These very large screen lengths are usually reserved for engineered prints.)

Rotary-screen printing The standard circumference for a screen is twenty-five, twenty-eight, thirty-two, thirty-six, or forty inches. The unit-length can be equal to or a divisor of any of these measurements.

Transfer printing The cylinders that are used to print the transfer paper have circumferences of 18½, 23⅝, and 27¹⁄₆ inches. The unit-length can be equal to or divisors of any of these measurements.

TROUBLE-SHOOTING

The following are errors that occur frequently with beginning attempts at doing a repeat. They are discussed here so that you can be on the lookout and avoid them in your own work.

A common mistake many beginning designers make when developing their first repeat is to use a single motif to do the job required by an entire repeat unit of motifs. Although a single motif can be put into repeat, the practice is usually viewed by professionals as a mistake. It indicates either a lack of understanding of the requirements of a repeat unit or insensitivity to the compositional requirements of design for printed textiles.

Another classic example of a repeat error is the development of a picture image into repeat layout. This is similar to the error of using a single motif; but here a picture composition is developed within the boundaries of four straight edges and put into a repeat system without regard for the interlocking of units or the relationship of compositional elements from one unit to the next. The images are plunked down next to each other, reading as individual and separate units.

These errors occur frequently because individuals have an understanding of the repeat systems without fully understanding the concept of the interlocking unit. If the repeat layout is to be successful, the units must be thought of as having a continuous flow that creates a larger pattern.

The repeat layout is successful when the repeat system is secondary to the design elements incorporated in it. A well-designed layout is one in which the system and repeated motifs are not obviously noticeable. In that occasional instance when a designer chooses to make a system intentionally noticeable, the effect must enhance the total pattern.

To get a better understanding of the repeat, spend a day in a store looking at printed fabrics. For each design, determine the unit and its length and width measurements; find the length repeat and the side repeat and decide what type of system is being used. Find repeated motifs. Your first encounter with creating a repeat layout may be a bit perplexing; but, the more exposure you have had to printed patterns, and the more experience with analyzing them, the easier your encounters will become.

Color is one of the most—if not *the* most—important aesthetic elements in a design. It is color that attracts first interest in a fabric then entices one to take a closer look at the cloth. It is an important factor in determining a person's like or dislike of the cloth and the designed printed on it. Through the good use of color, otherwise inferior designs have been produced and sold.

What distinguishes good color in textiles? This question must be weighed from the different viewpoints of the manufacturer, the consumer, and the creative textile designer. Each uses different criteria for determining the answer.

When considering what distinguishes good color from the viewpoint of the manufacturer or converter, one point prevails: good color is marketable color. Stylists working for converting houses spend a good deal of time

CHAPTER SEVEN

Color in textiles

researching what these salable colors will be. They consult many resources before making final decisions in coloring a new design or line of fabrics.

The resources that the stylist may turn to for direction are varied. There are several companies whose main function is to predict future trends in color as well as new looks in cloth design. The stylist may turn to one or more of these. Most of the major fiber manu-

facturers (there are several) also present color forecasts and distribute color swatches. Good stylists are aware of general moods and directions that emerge from within the market. They develop strong intuitive feelings about color direction through awareness and understanding of their particular market.

In the apparel fabrics industry, color changes rapidly. Color trends and new color looks are forecast twice a year and new designs with new colorings appear equally often. Color is forecast in advance of the time it appears on the retail market. New color direction is given a year or more in advance of the time it comes into the stores. What is considered correct color one season may be considered incorrect the next.

The furnishings fabric industry also has trends in color, but changes occur at a much slower pace. Here salable *colorways* can last for several years. The life of the original design may last years longer, by reprinting it in new colors that correspond to current trends. This recoloring can happen several times in the life of a design.

The area of the market to which the fabric will be sold is also considered when developing color looks. Whether it be for apparel or furnishing fabric, the use of color in the high-fashion market is generally more sophisticated.

From the consumer's point of view, correct color is the color that the individual likes best. But a favorite or desired color for one occasion may be different from the one desired for another. What colors come to mind when you think of babies, weddings, elections? Our selection of colors for each event is predictable as a result of cultural conditioning. Any of these same questions posed to an individual from a different cultural background will more than likely yield a different response. And likes and dislikes of color are unquestionably based on what we are acccustomed to or familiar with.

The creative textile designer must learn to choose and use color more objectively. Here a formal understanding of the principles of color is necessary. This is obtained through the study and practice of color theory. Some of the basic principles of color are outlined at the end of this chapter; but a more in-depth study of a particular color system may be beneficial to you.

The study of color theory will serve as a basis for understanding and using color in an enlightened way. It is not meant to standardize the results you achieve with color, but to help you achieve the particular color effects you want. A foundation in theory does not mean that you should ignore your intuitive sense of color, which will certainly be the basis for developing your own personal approach to color use. Rather, the understanding of theory should help you develop and realize this intuitive sense in the most skillful and purposeful way.

What is meant by purposeful use of color? It is a use that extends beyond mere surface decoration. A designer who understands the formal principles of color can use it to direct the viewer's eye over the surface of the cloth, thus conveying a sense of movement. Or for another example, color may be used to create an illusion of transparency or of special depth.

TEXTILE COLORING IN THE INDUSTRY

To allow the buyer a choice of colors when selecting fabrics, most designs are printed in more than one *colorway*. In the apparel fabrics trade, it is not uncommon for a design to be printed and sold in four or more colorways simultaneously. If the design runs over several seasons, new colorings will usually be made for each new season. As you can probably imagine, a design that enjoys a long run may be colored many times.

2a

2b

2c

2d

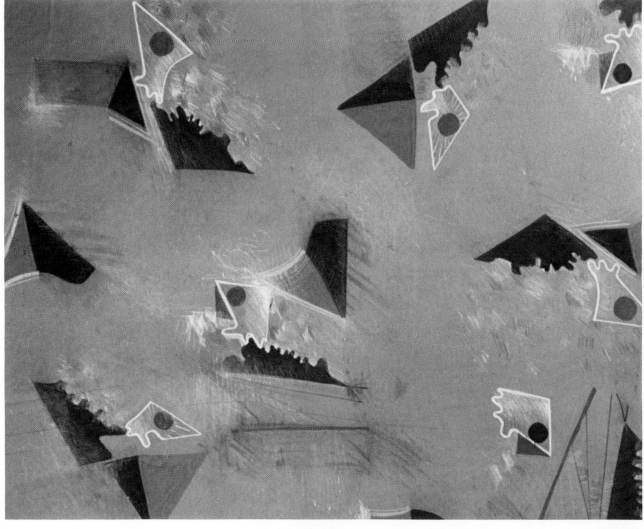

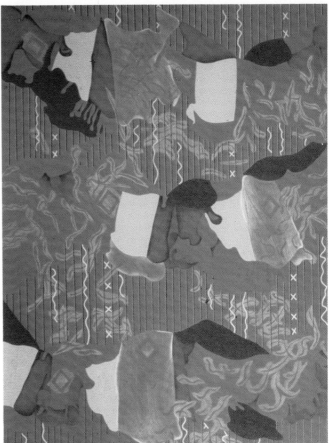

PREVIOUS PAGE
Plate 3 (above)
CAROLYN RAY
Evy
(Offset repeat: unit length 25¼"; unit width 17")
© 1980, Carolyn Ray.

Automatic flat-bed printed, seven screens, 52¼"
width.
Plate 4 (below)
GRACE DUNKAS
Sunset Series: IV
(Croquis; gouache and pencil, 16½" x 21½")
© 1980, Grace Dunkas.

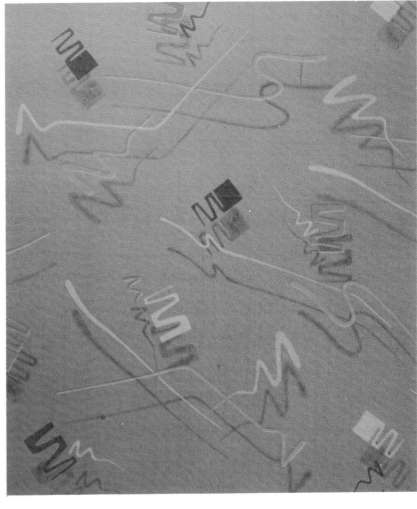

THIS PAGE
Plate 5 (above left)
MICHELLE DESVEAUX
Moving Parts
(Croquis; gouache, 9" x 12")
© 1979, Michelle Desveaux.

Plate 6 (above right)
MARCIA JEPSKY
Blue Ruffle
(Croquis; gouache and pencil, 19½" x 25½")
© 1980, Marcia Jepsky.

Plate 7 (right)
TERRY A. GENTILLE
Flouis
(Croquis; gouache and pencil, 17½" x 15¼")
© 1979, Terry A. Gentille.

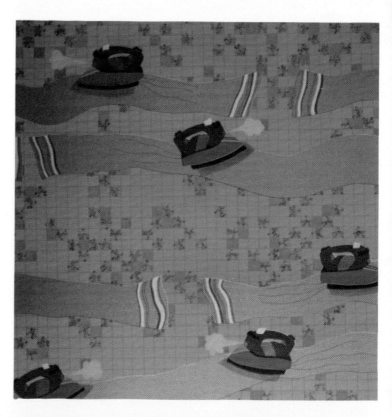

Plate 8 (right)
SUSAN GLASSER
Ironing Day
(Croquis; gouache and pencil, 20" x 18½")
© 1980, Susan Glasser.

Plate 9 (below)
FEDE CHETI
Alberini
(Detail of fabric; repeat not shown. Repeat length: 35")
© 1981, Groundworks, Inc. Fabric courtesy Patricia Green.

An original Fede Cheti design, produced and styled by
Groundworks, Inc. Automatic flat-bed printed, nine
screens, 52" width.

OPPOSITE PAGE
Plate 10
MARCIA JEPSKY
Indian Blanket No. 1
(Croquis; gouache, 14" x 30¾")
© 1981, Marcia Jepsky.

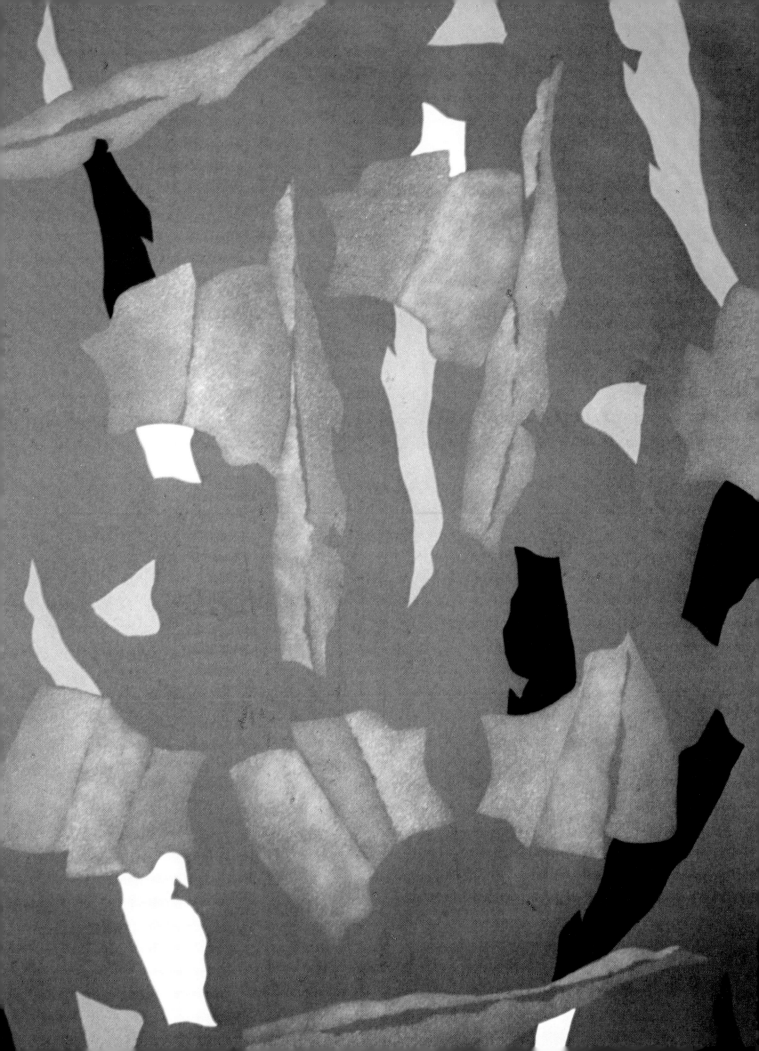

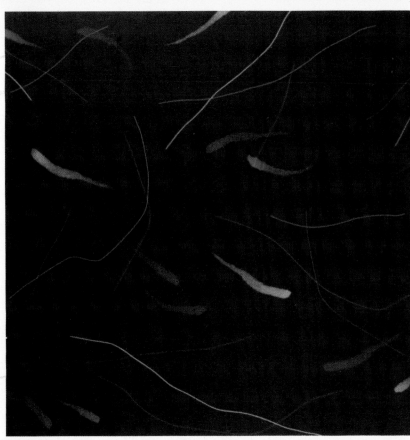

Plate 11
TERRY A. GENTILLE
Laser Lights Series: Comets
(Croquis; gouache, 19" x 19")
© 1979, Terry A. Gentille.

Plate 12
JENNIFER S. ORKIN
Egyptian Tracks
(Croquis; gouache, 16½" x 20½")
© 1981, Jennifer S. Orkin

Converters initially develop for each design a group of stock colorways that are available to their clients in quantities as large or small as required. Occasionally a design that is already in production will be reprinted in colors of the client's own choosing. When this kind of custom service is performed, the client is either required to buy a minimum number of yards or pay a high price for a limited length.

Colorists are people who develop colorings. A coloring is a section of the original design hand-painted in new colors. Colorings are used during printing for matching colors on the fabric to those in the painting.

In developing a set of colorings, a colorist first establishes a color look. This color look may be taken directly from the original croquis or newly developed according to the converter's own color direction. Once the color look has been established, successive colorings are painted. Apparel fabrics generally maintain the same feeling and color weight in all colorings. In furnishings, however, successive colorings are often dramatically different from one to another.

The number of colors used in a design will vary depending on several factors: the company, the market to which the fabric will be sold, and the type of printing method used. Fabrics directed to the mass market and volume sales usually have from one to eight colors. Each color in a design will increase the cost of the final product. Fabrics intended for a higher-priced market do not have these color restrictions: the number of colors can be upwards of fifteen. Because of their high cost, these fabrics go to a very specialized market.

Although new colorings of a design are occasionally done by the designer, more often they are prepared by the colorist. It is usually difficult for beginning designers to envision their designs in other colors, and at times, even more difficult to accept that other people may develop colorings for their designs. Of course, the initial colors in which a design is created are extremely important; but the designer should consider other coloring alternatives even in the very early stages of designing. You may even find it helpful to do several colorings of the same design to get a better idea of what happens to it when translated into new colors.

PAINTING A COLORING

The best way to develop a coloring is by repainting a section of the original design large enough to give an accurate impression of the design in new colors. This section must include one or more color areas for each of the colors used in the original design.

Start by drawing a square on a sheet of tracing paper equal to the size of the area that you will recolor. Make an accurate tracing of the original design with pencil in the squared area (see "Tracings and Rub-Downs," page 57). If the area from which you are working contains a lot of small details, you may want to leave them out of the tracing stage and later paint them directly onto the coloring. Once the tracing is complete, prepare a backing. You will use this backing for transferring successive outlines of the traced area for each new coloring that you paint.

The coloring should be rendered in exactly the same manner as the original croquis. If the original has a textural area, the coloring must duplicate it. Flat areas in the design must be painted flat in the coloring, and so forth. In printing, each color in the design equals a separate screen or roller. There will be no change in quality of texture, width of line, or size of shape. These factors are established as constant once the screen or roller is made. The coloring must retain these same constants to ensure the most accurate impression of the new colorway to be printed.

When transposing the design into new colors, all areas of a particular color must be changed into the same new color. That is to say, if, for example, the original croquis has red appearing at various points in the design, and in the new coloring you change red to blue, all red color positions must be changed to blue. You cannot change some red positions to blue and other red positions to green because all positions of the same color are printed by one roller and a roller can be only one color. Count the number of colors in the original croquis before mixing paint. You will need to mix a new color for each color position in the croquis.

Wet paint appears slightly different in color from dry paint. Paint a color tab on a strip of scrap paper as you mix each color to check its appearance when dry. Once all colors are mixed, paint a quick color *mock-up*, which approximates a small section of the coloring. This will enable you to see how the colors appear when painted in relationship to each other. You may need to do some color balancing at this point.

One color problem can arise simply from getting too close: When creating designs and colorings we become accustomed to seeing the colors from a foot or two away. But exciting color relationships that are apparent from up close may be lost when viewed from further away because the colors do not separate from each other. This has been a disappointing discovery for many beginning designers after devoting hours of work to a piece. Stand back and see how your color reads from a distance.

Color Balancing

Color balancing is the process of adjusting your colors so that each will relate properly to the other colors in the design. Although a painted color tab may appear correct when seen on its own, the same color may appear completely different when painted adjacent to other colors. Balancing a color may mean adding a few drops of white to lighten the value or a drop of black to darken it. The color may appear too blue or may need to be a little less red when compared to other colors. These subtle adjustments can only be made when all the colors in a coloring are painted adjacent to each other. The changes that you need to make will become apparent through painting the mock-up.

Try the following experiment to help better understand this principle. Paint a square of brilliant green on a black ground and then on a white ground. Use the same size square and the same size piece of ground paper. Position the square in the middle of the page. Notice that the brilliant green appears lighter and brighter on the black ground. The very same green, on the white ground, appears much darker. In each instance the color of the ground affects the appearance of the value and intensity of green.

Next try balancing the green used for

the black ground so that it will appear the same as the green on the white ground. This can be achieved by mixing a small amount of black paint into the green and repainting the square on another piece of black ground paper. Black paint must be added to the green paint a little at a time to ensure that the color does not become too dark. Make intermediate color tabs on black paper to check the green color as it is being darkened. Once you have mixed a new green that appears the same when painted on a black ground as the green painted on the white ground, you have successfully balanced the color.

Try balancing different color squares on different color grounds to further your understanding of the principles of color balancing. The following discussion of basic color theory should help you in determining how to change the value or intensity of a given color.

BASIC COLOR THEORY

Color is a property of light reflection. When we see color our eye is responding to a light wavelength reflecting from whatever that object may be. When white light is passed through a prism it is broken up into the rainbow hues which make our spectrum; this demonstrates that white light contains all color.

An object that appears yellow is absorbing all the color rays except yellow rays, which are reflected to our eye. Red or blue objects absorb all the color rays except red or blue ones. An object that appears black is absorbing all color rays while an object that appears white is reflecting all of them.

Properties of Color

The properties of color include hue, value, and intensity. An understanding of these will help you in mixing color and working with pigments.

HUE

Hue is the most essential characteristic of color. It refers to the name given to a particular color. Red, yellow, blue, green, and orange are hues.

The color wheel (Figure 7.1) is the most common structure for organizing color. The color wheel with which we are concerned applies to pigment, not light. The wheel contains twelve hues consisting of three primary colors, three secondary colors, and six tertiary colors.

The primary colors are yellow, blue and red. These three colors are used to make all other hues.

The secondary colors are orange, which is a mixture of the primary colors red and yellow; green which is a mixture of the primary colors yellow and blue; and violet, which is a mixture of the primary colors red and blue.

The tertiary colors, which are the mixtures of one primary color and an adjacent secondary color, are yellow-green, blue-violet, red-orange, red-violet, blue-green, and yellow-orange.

VALUE

Value refers to the lightness or darkness of a hue. When using pigment, the value of a hue can be lightened by adding white paint, or darkened by adding black. A lightened value is referred to as a *tint*, and a darkened value is referred to as a *shade*. Pink is a tint of red

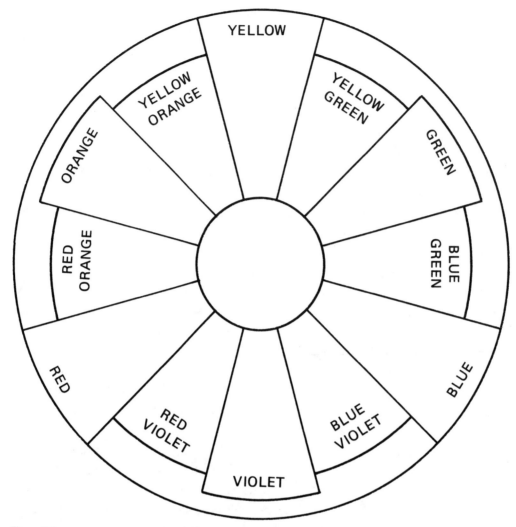

Figure 7.1
The color wheel.

while maroon is a shade of red; sky blue and navy blue are a tint and shade of blue.

INTENSITY

Intensity refers to the brightness or dullness of a hue. A color at full intensity contains little or no gray or is free of mixture with its complement. When using pigment, the intensity of a color can be dulled or neutralized by mixing it with its complement.

A color's complementary color is the color directly across from it on the color wheel. The complementary color of red is green, orange is blue, red-violet is yellow-green, and red-orange is blue-green. When complements are mixed in equal amounts they neutralize each other and produce gray. Complementary colors will intensify in brightness when placed next to each other and create an optical effect know as *vibration*.

The following exercises will help you achieve a better understanding of the properties of color and how they work when mixing pigments:

Mix a few drops of white into a color and paint a tab. Add a few drops more white and paint another tab. Continue adding white and painting tabs until you reach the color's lightest tint. Repeat the exercise to find the color's darkest shade by adding black. This will give you a good understanding of how to work with the full range of value of a color.

Try the same exercise, but this time change the intensity of a color by adding a few drops of its complement. Paint tabs and add more complementary color until the original hue has become neutralized.

Color Schemes

Color schemes can be helpful in planning the visual effects of a design. They are extremely useful in creating colorings when you are trying to give the same design a totally new visual impression. The four basic color schemes (often called *color harmonies*) are called *monochromatic, analogous, complementary,* and *triadic.*

A monochromatic color schemes employs only one hue, which may be used in variations of value and intensity.

An analogous color scheme combines adjacent colors on the color wheel: the combination of blue-green, blue, and blue-violet is an example. Within this scheme, the hue may change in value and intensity.

A complementary color scheme combines colors opposite each other on the color wheel. The colors may change in intensity and value.

A triadic color scheme is one that combines three hues that are equally spaced on the color wheel. The combination of red, yellow, and blue would be an example.

Color Factors

LIGHT

Colors are affected by the light under which they are seen. If the light changes, the color will also change. View your designs both under your work light and in daylight.

DISTANCE

This factor should be considered in creating a design: Color observed from very close will appear different when viewed from a greater distance. A design should be viewed from near and far before deciding on the final color look.

SPECIAL ILLUSIONS

Warm, intense colors, such as yellow, orange, and red, appear to advance (aggressive colors); cooler colors, such as green and blue, appear to recede (retiring colors). With this knowledge, the designer can create interesting illusions of space.

COLOR RELATIONSHIPS

A color is always seen in relationship to another color or colors. The hue, value, and intensity of a color can appear to change depending on the effects of background or adjacent colors. The amount of color will also affect the way we see it and its relationship to another color. Moreover, the design painted in several colors can be repainted with the same colors and yet appear quite different if their positions within the design are changed.

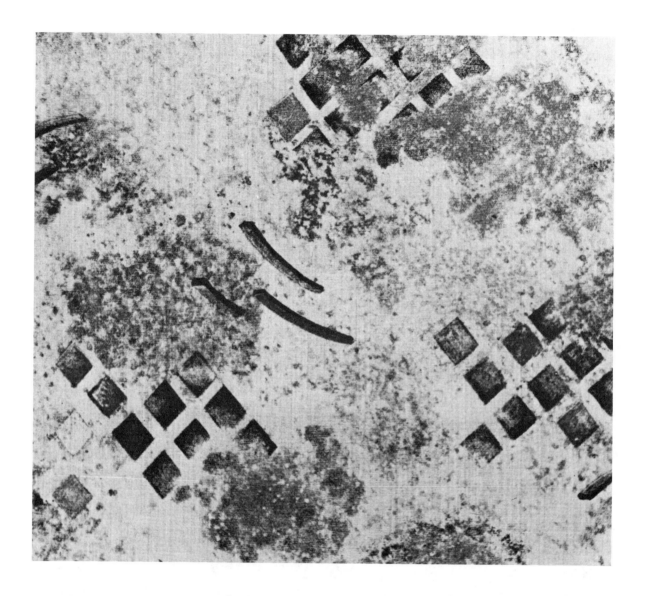

Every design, no matter how complex, can be printed. Not all designs, however, can be printed by every method. Certain printing methods are more conducive to certain types of design technique.

It need not be emphasized that the designer for printed textiles must be conversant with the capabilities of each method. The way in which your concept is to be reproduced can influence dramatically the ultimate success of the design. Obviously, the better you understand the requirements of printing, the better able you will be to prepare your designs for repeat and manufacturing.

A faithful reproduction of a design onto cloth depends on the ability of the engraving

CHAPTER EIGHT

Industrial printing processes

artist to accurately reproduce it for transfer onto rollers or screens. The quality of the printer's work is another determining factor in successfully transposing the design from paper to cloth.

The base cloth on which the design is printed will also affect reproduction. A fine-lined design, for instance, will reproduce fairly accurately on silk or cotton broadcloth, but lose much of its detail if printed on velvet or corduroy.

A stylist takes these points into consideration when choosing a design for a particular house. Converters often specialize in printing on a particular base cloth, such as cotton or silk, as well as specializing in one

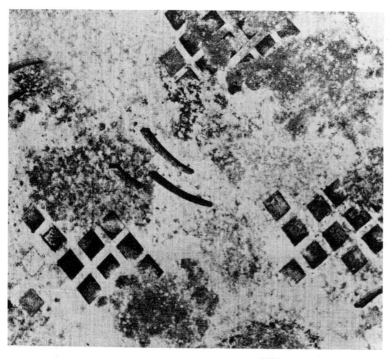

Figure 8.1
Roller printed fabric, detail.
Courtesy of Mr. Condotti Ltd., New York.

printing method, such as screen printing or roller printing. A specialty house may use many different base cloths and printing methods to develop their fabrics.

Following is a description of the most important printing processes. To supplement your reading, it would be helpful for you to collect fabrics printed with each process so that you will have a better understanding of what is achievable through each.

ROLLER PRINTING

The roller machine consists of a series of copper rollers positioned around a large,

main cylinder roller. Each roller is engraved with the design elements of one color from the design in repeat. If the design has eight colors, eight separate rollers will be engraved. Roller printing machines can print up to fourteen colors.

Prepared for printing, the cloth passes around the main cylinder and makes contact with the engraved rollers. The engraved rollers print the different colors simultaneously onto the cloth. Each engraved roller is supplied continuously with pigment or dye by a second roller, the color furnisher, as the fabric is being printed. Excess color is scraped from the roller by the *doctor blade*.

The rollers are engraved by etching in the same manner that plates for paper print etchings are produced. Very fine lines, *half-tones*, and subtle-to-bold textures are among the many delicate effects achievable in roller printing. In fact, the wonderful engraving potential of this method is often under-utilized.

Roller printing can produce up to one hundred yards of printed fabrics a minute, depending on the complexity of design and the number of rollers used. But because of the expense and time involved in setting up a machine, this is not a practical method for printing short runs.

SCREEN PRINTING

Screen printing is a modified stencil process. Screens are made from a meshed material of woven metal, nylon or polyester filament, or—rarely used today—silk. The design in repeat is transferred to the screens by blocking out all areas except the shapes to be printed. The blocking out is often achieved through photochemical processes.

As in roller printing, each screen prints all the design elements of the same color in the repeat. If the design has ten colors, ten separate screens will be made, one for each color. Once the screens are made, registration is checked to make sure that all the color areas will fit together and give an accurate reproduction of the design. During printing, the pigment or dye paste is pushed through

the non-blocked areas of the screen by a rubber blade, called a *squeegee*.

Three types of production screen printing are used in the industry: hand printing, automatic flat-bed printing, and rotary-screen printing. Although the basic process is the same for all three types, there are some major differences between them, involving automation, printing time, the number of colors that can be printed, and maximum repeat length that can be used.

Hand Printing

In hand printing, the screen material is stretched over a frame with block-out material adhered to it, and the stencil is made. During printing, the cloth which has been prepared for printing is stretched on a long, flat, padded table. To print the first color, the screen is placed on the cloth, print paste is poured on the inside edge of the screen, and the squeegee is pulled across it. The print paste moves in front of the squeegee while at the same time being pushed through the screen openings and onto the fabric. Once this process is completed, the screen is lifted and moved into the next printing position. The process is repeated until the entire length of the fabric is completed and all colors are printed.

Hand printing is slower that other screen methods, but it allows you short print runs, long repeat lengths, and numerous colors: Designs containing twenty-five colors and more have been printed with this method.

Figure 8.2
Top view of a rotary-screen printing machine.
Photograph courtesy of Cranston Print Works Company.

Fabric is moved automatically forward between rotary screens and
backing belt. Unprinted fabric is seen background left; printed
cloth is in right foreground.

Figure 8.3
Transfer-printed fabric, detail.

Automatic Flat-Bed Printing

This method of printing is similar to hand printing, but the screens and squeegees are operated automatically. The cloth is moved forward on a moving backing-belt while the screen is automatically raised and lowered in place.

About seven yards of fabric can be printed each minute. The advantage of this method is that it increases levels of speed and accuracy of the printing while still allowing for long repeat lengths.

The number of colors will vary depending on the length of the repeat and printing facilities. It is possible to print up to twenty colors for a repeat of approximately fifty-three inches.

Rotary-Screen Printing

In rotary-screen printing, the screens are large cylinders that rotate. The squeegee, positioned inside the cylinder, pushes the color through the screen openings and onto the fabric. The print paste is automatically fed into the screen's interior. The fabric is moved forward on a moving backing-belt.

Rotary printing allows for larger repeat sizes than roller printing but offers the same speed, up to one hundred yards per minute. Short runs are possible and screens, although more fragile than copper rollers, are less expensive to make. Up to twelve colors can be printed.

TRANSFER PRINTING

Transfer printing, also known as *Sublistatic* printing, involves the transfer of a design, which has first been printed on coated paper with sublimable dyes, onto cloth. During transfer, which takes place under heat and pressure, the dyes sublimate, turning directly from the solid state into vapor, and fix themselves into the fiber.

The design is prepared for printing onto the transfer paper in much the same fashion that designs are prepared for rollers or screens. First, working from the design in repeat, color separations are made by a separation artist. The separations are used to engrave the design onto cylinders. The cylinders, in turn, are used to print the transfer paper.

When designs are extremely complicated or difficult to separate by hand, they are photographed using the four-color separation process. In this process, each color in the design is broken down into the three primary colors plus black. The transfer paper is printed in these four colors. This process is basically the same method used for reproducing a color photograph in a magazine. It insures an exact reproduction of the design in repeat. The major drawback of the four-color separation process is that the types of different colorways you can make from the original design are very limited.

With transfer printing, any type of design technique can be duplicated. Depending on

the type of engraving, unlimited colors may be used. Once the transfer paper is printed the transfer of the design onto cloth is very fast, and short runs are practical.

DISCHARGE PRINTING

Although discharge printing utilizes a screen or roller, the process of coloring the cloth is different from that of direct screen or roller printing. In discharge printing, the color is bleached out of the base cloth and simultaneously replaced with another color. The cloth is first piece-dyed with dischargeable (removable) dyes; the design is then printed with dyes mixed with a discharging agent. It is also possible to discharge color from the piece-dyed cloth without replacing it. This might be done, for example, to show the ground cloth for a two-color print.

Discharge printing insures that the design will have excellent fit. It is especially useful when large areas of blotched-color ground are desired in a design.

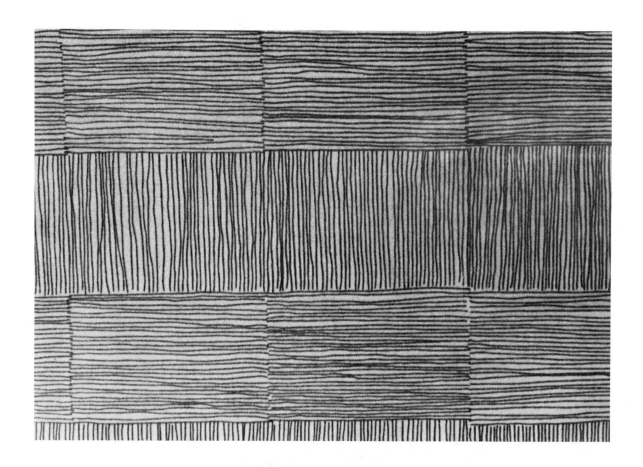

The content of your textile design port-folio will vary depending on the type of work you are seeking. A portfolio used for obtaining a full-time position within a company would be different from one that is developed for obtaining freelance work.

A job portfolio, one developed to obtain a position working in a design studio or converting house, should include a variety of finished designs in croquis form, repeats, and colorings. These should demonstrate your color, design, and technical capabilities, as well as the types of hands in which you are able to work. The work should be creative

CHAPTER NINE

Professional practices

and distinctive, reflecting a strong, personal direction and point of view about design on cloth.

The second type of portfolio, developed to solicit freelance work, should include a group of series of designs in croquis form. Each series, containing six to ten designs, must show specific design direction. This type of portfolio is called a *collection*.

In the textile business, collections are developed three or four times a year. It is not uncommon for a collection developed for the apparel trade to have a hundred or more designs. Collections developed for the fur-

Figure 9.1A
JASON POLLEN
Untitled Series (croquis, watercolor and collage,
7″ × 7″).
Copyright © 1979, Jason Pollen.

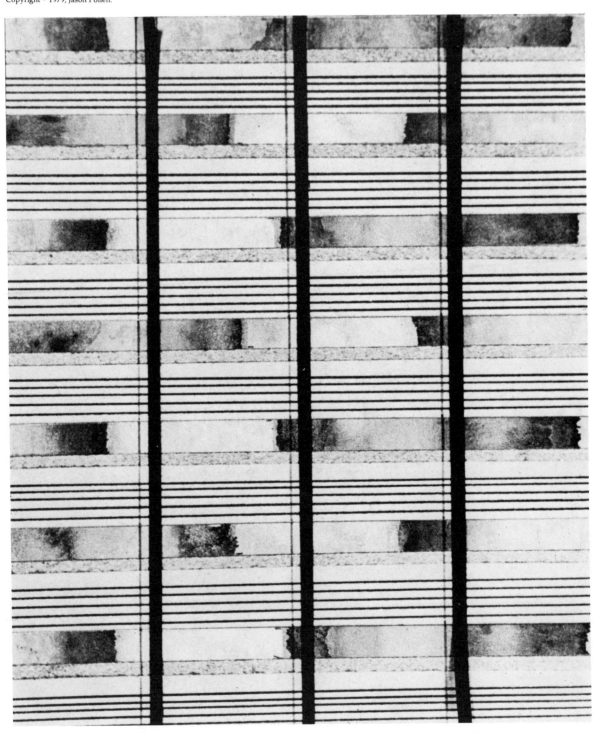

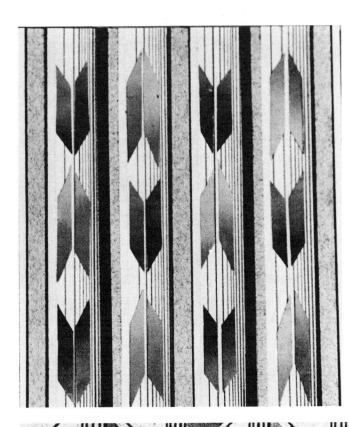

Figure 9.1B
JASON POLLEN
Untitled Series (croquis, watercolor and collage,
4½″ × 5½″).
Copyright © 1979, Jason Pollen.

Figure 9.1C
JASON POLLEN
Untitled Series (croquis, watercolor and collage,
5″ × 6″).
Copyright © 1979, Jason Pollen.

Figures 9.1A, B, and C are three designs from the
same series.

nishings trade generally tend to have a smaller number of designs.

It is important that your collection portfolio be developed to show a variety of series, each series indicating a different design conviction. The collection should not be a potpourri of designs without focus. The ability to develop a collection in series form is unquestionably the mark of a good professional designer.

Presentation

The way in which you present your designs is almost as important as the quality of the work itself. Presentation is a reflection of the designer's attitude toward his or her own work. Good presentation may influence the attitude of a buyer in a positive way; poor presentation can do just the opposite.

Prospective employers and buyers of designs generally look through a portfolio very quickly, often pausing no longer than four or five seconds to view a piece of work. Your presentation should thus facilitate rapid examination while ensuring that your work is shown to its best advantage.

MOUNTING YOUR DESIGNS

Designs should be mounted on clean, white, lightweight mount paper. Use a consistent mount size for all work, even though the sizes of the actual designs may vary. A standard-size sheet of lightweight paper, 22½ × 28½ inches, works well for designs of average size. Bigger mounts will be needed if work is larger in scale. Do not be afraid to have a lot of mount showing around the design; this will only enhance your presentation.

Mounting designs on the same size paper will facilitate your presentation because turning designs, like turning pages of a book, seems easier where there is uniformity. It is of visual importance as well: Designs are generally piled on top of each other when they are being shown; if they have different mount sizes, the edges of the larger designs will show behind the smaller ones and interfere visually with the smaller designs.

The design should be attached so that its top is parallel to the shortest measurement of the mount, usually 22½ inches (see Figure 9.2). Use a small amount of rubber cement on the back of each corner of the design. Apply the cement sparingly; if the mount becomes dirty or torn, the design will need to be removed and remounted on clean paper.

To separate the mount from the design, stick a butter knife between them and move it back and forth in a sawing motion from the inside of the glued corner to the corner tip. Keep the flat of the blade parallel between the papers. (See Figure 9.3.)

For the sake of the basic quality of your presentation, carry your designs in a case large enough so that all can lie flat. Never roll designs. If showing a portfolio several times in the same day, carry a kneaded eraser with you, to make on-the-spot cleaning touchups, if needed, between appointments.

If you are showing a collection of designs created in series, present each series in its own individual paper folder. Folders can be made by taping two sheets of mount paper together and folding the covers together so that the tape is on the inside.

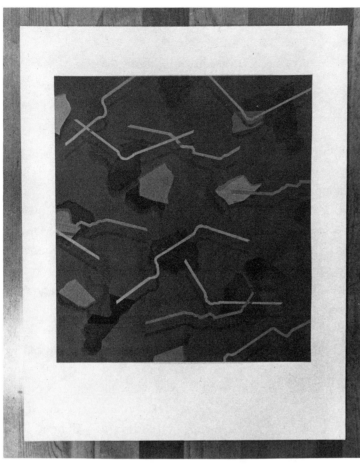

A croquis correctly placed on a mount.

Figure 9.3 (below)
Removing a design from a damaged
mount. Butter knife is moved forward
in a sawing motion from inside of
glued corner to corner tip.

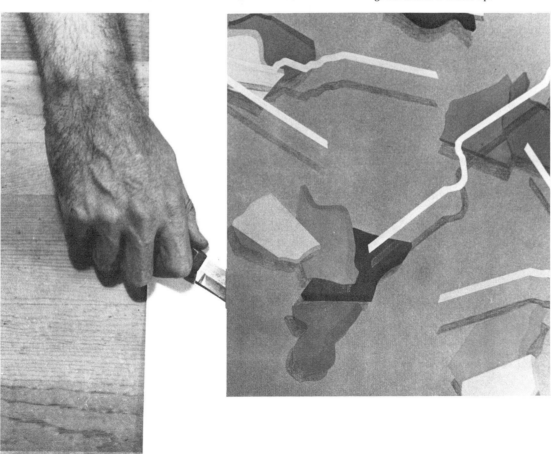

PROFESSIONAL SITUATIONS

The Design Studio

A design studio is usually composed of several designers working under the direction of a studio director, who is often the owner of the studio. Design studios produce work on paper only: croquis, repeats, and colorings. They do not become involved with the actual production of the printed fabric. The general design direction of a studio is generally developed by the director. The director will then work with the designers as each collection is developed.

Collections are usually created on a speculative basis and taken into the market by a studio salesperson. Commissioned work is also done by some studios. The amount of work done on commission compared to that done on speculation will vary from studio to studio.

Designers working for a studio may be paid a weekly salary that is considered a draw against the sales of their designs, or they may be paid only when their designs have sold. The studio takes a percentage of the sale price of the design and the designer receives the rest. Designers are usually expected to furnish their own brushes and other tools.

The advantage of working in a design studio is that it offers a structured working environment with other designers. It provides design direction and motivation from the studio director, and a sales representative to sell your designs. The right design studio can offer an excellent learning atmosphere for beginning designers.

The disadvantage is that there is, depending upon the studio, often a lack of creative freedom and almost always a lack of personal recognition. In some studios, uncertain weekly wages may also be a problem.

The Converting Studio

A converter is involved with the whole process of creating a textile, from croquis to sale of the completed cloth to the manufacturer. Most converters have in-house design studios, directed by stylists who determine overall design direction.

Most converting studios buy their original designs from freelance designers and design studios. Designers working in the converting studio may then be called upon to reinterpret these designs to suit house needs. In some instances the designs will need to be greatly changed. Converters' designers also may do repeat work, coloring, and mill work—supervising and approving of fabrics during printing. Smaller converting houses may have only one or two designers to do all these jobs, while large houses often have people who specialize in each of these areas.

The type of pattern printed by a converter, its quality of printing, and originality of design will vary widely. These factors are determined by the vision of the company, the price of the fabric and the area of the market to which it is sold. Designs for expensive fabrics, which go to a limited market, can be more innovative than those for the mass market, which may be less inspired.

Designers working in the studio are supplied with all tools and materials and given studio space. The advantages of working in a converting studio are exposure to all phases of fabric production and marketing approaches, and set weekly wages. One can receive a good introduction to the field and excellent technical training in the right house.

The major disadvantage is again lack of creative freedom. If original work is developed in a converting studio, the designer rarely receives recognition for it. Designers working in this kind of situation for too long a time may begin to lose their own artistic identities.

Freelancing

Freelancing is working for yourself. You are your own boss, set your own hours, and can have total artistic control over the creation of your designs. But you must also establish enough business to make a living.

Freelance designers usually create collections geared toward either the apparel or home furnishings market, although there are some designers who work in both areas. Similarly to design studios, some freelancers design only on a speculative basis, while others work totally or in part on commission.

The freelance designer may be represented by an agent, who gets a percentage of the sale price of the design. Alternatively, designers may represent themselves and take their own work into the market. This direct contact with clients is often stimulating and may cultivate ideas for potential design directions. However an agent can be very useful for contacts and business knowledge, and using one frees you to spend your time designing.

The rights to designs are conveyed in three ways: they can be sold outright, their reproduction rights can be sold, or they can be licensed for production. Licensing is undoubtedly the best way of getting work produced. The designer receives royalties while retaining ownership of the original art work.

The next best procedure is selling reproduction rights for a flat fee. Here the designer agrees to the production of the design in one area, such as home furnishings: drapery, upholstery, and wallpaper. But the designer still owns the original design and the rights to reproduce it in non-conflicting areas, such as apparel fabrics or domestics.

In selling a design outright, the designer agrees to relinquish any claim to the design's reproduction rights. This is unfortunately the most prevalent method of sale currently in practice—and the least acceptable to the designer.

The advantages compared to the disadvantages of freelancing are obvious. But success requires talent, perseverance, commitment, and long, hard hours.

FINDING YOUR MARKET

The criteria for designs that will be used for furnishings or apparel fabrics may or may not be different. Depending largely on the companies producing fabric and contemporary trends, many of your designs may be equally appropriate for the apparel and furnishings markets. Of course, not every design will serve all purposes. Discovering the market suitable for your work begins with discovering your own personal design direction. The creation of a portfolio representing your individual style is more important than creating designs that you think are directed toward a specific market. The preconceptions of designing for a specific market may be too limiting to a beginning designer's creativity. If the development of creative work is a priority, it seems logical to first create the work and then search for a market.

Finding companies that are interested in using your designs may take time. Familiarize yourself with the design looks of various companies by looking through fashion and interior design periodicals.

Ultimately, it's a matter of showing your designs to any and every kind of firm that uses printed fabrics. The most obvious buyer is the converter; but manufacturers of clothing—from designer names to loungewear—and furniture—from exclusive pieces to the interiors of mobile homes—often buy designs. Once you have discovered companies that like and use your work, and with which you like working, you have found your market.

BUSINESS PROCEDURES

The designer in the business world needs to establish proper business procedures. Understanding copyright, licensing, and other legal issues, as well as billing and record keeping, are important to good business practices.

The Textile Designers Guide, a discipline of the Graphic Artists Guild, is an organization committed to raising the ethical standards of the profession and establishing good busi-

ness practices. They can provide the designer with much important information concerning business procedures. Their address: 30 East 20th Street, New York, NY 10003.

Copyright

A copyright is the exclusive right to sell reproduction rights to a work of art. (There are, of course, other copyrightable categories of work, but our concern is only with copyrights for textile designs.)

On January 1, 1979, a new copyright law came into effect governing treatment of copyright for all work created after that date. Simply stated, the law provides that all creative, original work executed after January 1, 1979, is automatically protected by copyright as soon as it is created. All original textile designs that you produce will fall into this category.

You are the owner of the copyright to each design you create. Protection is secured by placing your copyright notification on each design. This will entitle you to sell reproduction rights—or limited reproduction rights—to the design while still retaining ownership of the copyright. The conditions of any sale of these rights should be negotiated by you and your buyer and then finalized in the form of a written, contractual agreement.

Further information about copyright can be obtained by sending for the free Copyright Information Kit from the Copyright

Office, Library of Congress, Washington, D.C., 20559, or from the Graphic Artists Guild.

Labeling Designs

Designs are named or numbered for invoicing purposes. Number designs in series order: 1001, 1002, and so forth. Each series begins a new sequence of numbers.

On each design should appear your name, the international copyright sign ©, the year date, and a title or design number. This information should appear on the center of the back of the design, and on the back of the mount. If you wish, you can also put this information on the front lower right corner.

Invoicing

When you sell a design, a written invoice with terms of the sale agreement or reproduction rights should be signed by the client. Never leave designs at any company without obtaining a signed invoice.

If a design is being held for consideration by a company, then a holding form, with terms of agreement, should be signed by the client. Designs should only be left for holding at companies with which you have experienced good working relationships or that you know to be reputable. Model forms for invoices and holding forms can be obtained from the Graphic Artists Guild.

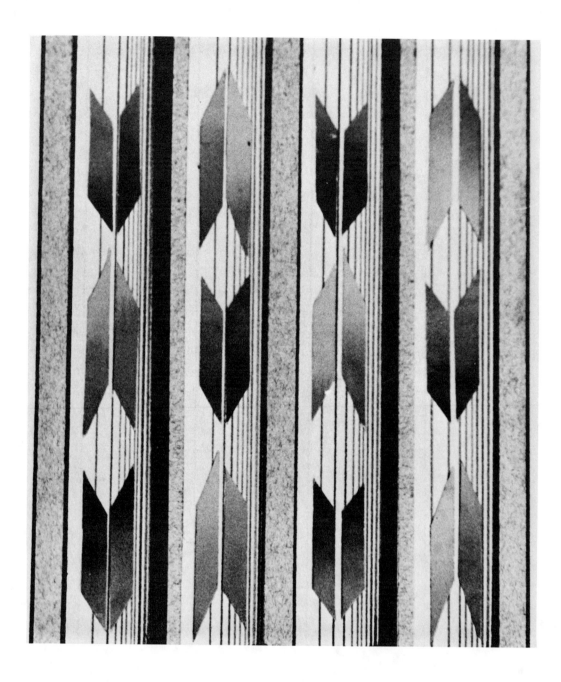

The projects in this section are offered so that the beginner may have the opportunity to go through some of the processes involved in developing a variety of basic designs for printed textiles. The exercises are presented in a sequence of increasing complexity and should therefore be undertaken in order.

Projects 1–5 will be particularly useful for discovering approaches to the development of new motifs and design imagery. In Project 1 you will make a complete visual investigation of an object in a series of drawings. You will then extract, reinterpret, and finally alter that idea to discover a fund of motif-developing techniques.

CHAPTER TEN

Ten
print-design projects

In Project 2 you will deal with two or more design images and their relationship to each other. Project 3 uses the croquis developed in Project 2 as a reference source for a coordinating design. In Project 4, you must progress from idea to croquis within a six-hour time limit.

Project 5 expands further your ability to develop motifs from ordinary sources of reference; in Projects 6, 7, and 8, you concern yourself with more expressive image development. (These projects should be undertaken only after you have gained familiarity with the requirements of the croquis.) The final two projects deal specifically with developing designs in a series and creating a repeat.

PROJECT 1

Find an organic object—a rock, a flower, an insect, a piece of honeycomb, or perhaps a dried leaf. Using pencil, inks, or any drawing medium you prefer, do a series of six drawings of your object. Turn the object in different directions and draw it from different angles and viewpoints. Observe and record the object's shape, form, and qualities of surface. Record any details that are characteristic of the particular object.

The purpose of doing these drawings is to help you make a thorough visual investigation of an object.

Once the drawings are complete, select the one you find most interesting and develop a motif from it by manipulating or changing its character. Do this by first selecting from the following list the word that suggests the greatest contrast to the qualities of your drawings. Then reinterpret the drawing according to the meaning that the word suggests to you.

burst	crack
blur	twist
cut	shatter
stretch	zigzag
coil	pierce
bend	distort

When reinterpreting the object according to the word, be sure to maintain all the characteristics that you originally recorded in the reference drawings. If, for example, you use the word *crack* in reinterpreting the organic-object drawings, make only changes in the motif-drawing that you feel are characteristic of *crack*. Be sure that you do not eliminate details or texture and that you do not simplify or stylize the reinterpreted motif drawing.

The purpose of doing this reinterpretation drawing is to discover methods of developing new and original motifs. Continue to use the same drawing medium, but you may now add two or three colors that are in some way related to the object you are working from.

Next, change the scale of the motif so that you have another motif, identical to the first, but either larger of smaller. All details of the motif are to remain constant except for scale change. Use at least two sizes of motifs. You may work with more if you like.

Once you have varying motif sizes and have read Chapter 5 on the croquis, develop on tracing paper a preliminary layout incorporating these different sizes. When developing this layout, be sure to consider the direction and density of the motifs.

When the preliminary layout is completed to your satisfaction, do a backing and make a rub-down onto a ground paper. Complete all motifs in the design by duplicating the different-sized interpreted motifs from which you are working. Once all motifs are completed, the finished croquis is achieved.

PROJECT 2

Choose two or more objects that you either have with you on your person or that can be found in your immediate vicinity. Try to select things that you would not ordinarily consider as inspirational for a printed textile design. You might choose a pair of glasses or shoes, scissors or a pencil, a light fixture, or perhaps a chair.

Do a page or more of drawings from these objects using any color medium. The drawings should be developed according to the compositional requirements of the croquis. This means that sketches of the objects should be recurring on the page and be composed in relationship to one another. The composition of the design should indicate how the sketched object would continue if expanded beyond the edges of the paper. The edge of the page is irrelevant to the compositional considerations of the drawing.

Interpret your objects in any style of drawing that you deem appropriate. The drawings do not have to be realistic but should capture the essence or unique quality of each object.

You might consider one of the following ways to approach the drawings:

- Look at the objects from different viewpoints and perspectives, enlarging and shrinking their visual size, and drawing what you discover.

- Examine the objects very closely and for minute details: holes, curves, depressions, texture, and subtle color changes. The drawings can be developed directly from these details without recording the shape or form of the object.

- Look at the shadows that the objects cast, the relationship between them, and the surface they are on. Your drawings may only be concerned with shadow/surface relationships.

Once you have finished the drawing, you may choose to work from the entire page or use only an area that you find particularly interesting. Working from the drawing, create a preliminary croquis layout on tracing paper, make a backing, and do a rub-down onto ground paper.

Render the design in the same medium that was used for the original drawing. Retain the same approach to technique, character, and style in the croquis as was in the original drawing.

PROJECT 3

Working directly from the finished croquis that you developed in Project 2, create a new design that will coordinate with it so that the two related designs might be used together in the same garment or interior space. The new croquis should retain design characteristics established in the first pattern. Consider the following suggested techniques for creating a similar yet different design. You may use one or more of these in your new croquis, interchanging options in whatever way is suitable to your needs.

1. Maintain the same medium, drawing technique, and colors to develop a new set of motifs which are similar yet different from the first set. Use the same colors, but shift the color emphasis. For example, if red, pink, green, turquoise, and beige are used in the first design, and the predominant colors are red and pink, then in the coordinated croquis use turquoise and green as the pre-

dominating colors, with red, pink, and biege in less dominant color positions.

2. Use the same motifs in the coordinated croquis but create a new layout in which the density and positioning of motifs in relationship to one another are changed considerably from the first design. If, for example, the first croquis has motifs that are closely and evenly placed, the second croquis might have a less dense and irregular placement of motifs with large areas of ground.

3. Create a coordinating croquis using the same or adapted motifs but changed in scale. If, for example, the first design has large motifs, use very small motifs in its coordinate.

4. Use a new technique to develop motifs for the coordinated design. For example, create a design using the flush-joining technique to coordinate with a design created through the use of the ruling pen. To ensure that the designs relate to each other, maintain the same use of color and color predominance.

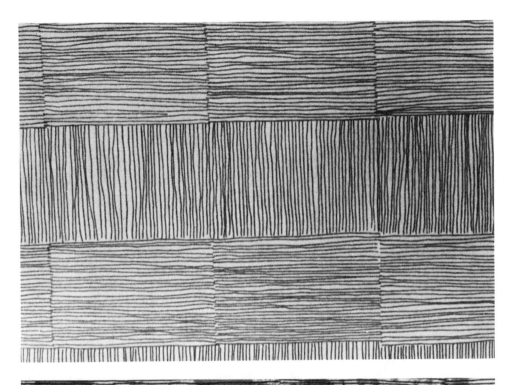

Figure 10.1A (left)
CAROLYN RAY
Peacock Feather (detail).
Copyright © 1978 by Carolyn Ray.

Hand screen printed, two screens, 53″ width.

Figure 10.1B (top)
CAROLYN RAY
Weave.
Copyright © 1978 by Carolyn Ray.

Hand screen printed, one screen, 44″ width.

Figure 10.1C
CAROLYN RAY
Venus IV (detail)
Copyright © 1978, Carolyn Ray.

Hand screen printed, two screens, 44″ width. Figures 10.1A, B, and and C are coordinated by color.

PROJECT 4

This project is oriented towards technique. Within a time limit of six hours, you are to progress from idea to completed croquis for a printed textile.

You may develop motifs from any reference source or from your imagination. The croquis must be a minimum of 11 × 14 inches; it may also be larger. And you must use one technique from each of the following groups:

Group 1	*Group 2*	*Group 3*
Flat Gouache	Shaded Pencil	Ruling Pen
Flush Joining	Stippling	Frisket
Drawing		Surface
Compass		Rubbings

In executing the techniques, work with—not against—the inherent characteristics and qualities unique to each. Do not, for instance, use the ruling pen to draw an outline that could be painted by hand. Use instead the ruled line of the ruling pen. This is the distinctive and special quality that should be incorporated into the croquis.

Each technique used in the croquis should also be an integral part of the design. It should be relevant to the total concept of the design and not be used merely to fulfill the requirements of the project.

Consider the limited time and required use of techniques before determining how you will approach the development of motifs, layout, or other design elements.

PROJECT 5

Select a reference that has many components: a car, bicycle, musical instrument, or electric food mixer would be good choices. Develop a series of color drawings isolating different areas of the reference.

For example, if your reference source is a bicycle, you might become interested in the spokes of the wheel, their relationship to the hub at one end, or the relationship to the wheel at the other. The next point of interest might concentrate on the pedals or chain. Continue exploring different parts of the bicycle by drawing each of its areas that interests you.

Next, do not return to the actual subject matter but work directly from the reference sketches, to develop motifs that are suggested by the drawings. The motifs can be developed by combining reference drawings and creating a totally new image or by further interpreting the drawings.

Create a croquis that combines more than one type of motif and is based on your reference drawings. Use as many colors and any media that seem appropriate to your drawings. Consider the layout possibilities, density of motifs, and motif direction; try a new approach to layout that you have not previously used.

Two other points to consider in designing the croquis are the development of equally interesting *positive* and *negative spaces* and the use of color within the motifs to create an illusion of spacial depth.

Be inventive with the information you have to work with.

PROJECT 6

Take a trip to any place that offers a new environmental experience or exposes you to something that you would not ordinarily see. You might go to a zoo, a park, a museum, or another town. Create a series of reference drawings at your chosen location.

Your reference sketches should include anything you find significant about the place that you visit. Draw inspiration from material to which you would not ordinarily be exposed, to develop motifs suitable for a croquis. The croquis should communicate a visual description of the location, or points of interest that you found there.

Be sure to pay attention to the basic design principles of layout, technique, and color within the croquis. A variety of techniques may be used to develop the motifs for the design, and you may also use up to twenty colors.

PROJECT 7

Create a croquis that expresses a mood, feeling, or emotion. Be prepared to explain how your uses of color, shape, and layout are related to the particular mood or emotion that you are expressing.

The feeling of tranquility, for instance, might be expressed through the use of soft or indistinct shapes. The color suggested by this feeling might be misty, pale tints of various hues. The layout could be of motifs sparsely placed on a pale tinted ground.

The interpretation of any feeling, mood, or emotion into concrete elements can, more than most design subjects, reveal aspects of the artist's character and personality. It is likely that different artists interpreting the same mood in a visual context would arrive at very different solutions.

PROJECT 8

Create a croquis based on a narrative. The story on which the motifs and design elements are based might be a personal life experience or historic event, or it might tell of some fantasy world or mythical time.

Consider the relevance of your design imagery to the context of the narrative. What significance do the individual motifs have to the story or event you are trying to express? How might you introduce meaning to the way images recur within the layout? What might your use of color have to do with the narrative? How might you use it to express a certain time or environmental quality?

Use these questions as guidelines and be prepared to answer them for yourself as you develop the croquis. Every aspect of the design should be considered both aesthetically and within the context of the story that you are narrating.

PROJECT 9

Create a group of three or more designs which work together as a series. Designs that work together this way are similar in feeling without being the same. As examples, see the three designs in series represented by Figures 9.1A, B, and C; or compare Figure 5.3 to Plate 7, shown in color.

Designs developed in a series do not need to be coordinated; in other words, they do not need to be designed so that they work together within the same interior space or used together on the same garment. They should, however, express a unified design conviction or personal design direction.

An example of a series would be a group of designs, in which each expresses a different quality of a sunset; or for a more prosaic example, a group could be created by interpreting different kitchen tools.

Different designs within the same series would use different layout considerations. Each one may have different considerations of density and motif direction. Compare for example the density of motifs in Figures 0.2 and 3.17 with that of Plate 4.

Designs within a series would also be different in color, although the approach to the way color is used might be similar. For example, in each design of a series colored in different hues, the values of the hues could be the same: Hues in pale tints might be used or dark shades of different hues might be used consistently through the series.

Designs in a series are usually created with the same techniques. Gouache and pencil might be the techniques used for rendering all designs in a series. The percentage of amounts of gouache to amounts of pencil technique might vary greatly from one design to another within the series.

PROJECT 10

Working from any of the croquis that you have developed in the preceding nine projects, prepare a repeat according to the aligned or offset repeat system. The repeat should be measured according to industrial repeat size specifications.

A preliminary repeat layout should first be made on tracing paper and should be squared with your T-square and triangle. The scale and compositional arrangement of the layout must remain the same as in the croquis from which you are working.

Glossary

aligned repeat. The system of positioning interlocking repeat units so that they are aligned both vertically and horizontally.

backing. A reverse tracing of the preliminary layout which, when rubbed down onto the ground paper, will produce the obverse image of the layout.

base cloth. The fabric on which the design is printed.

blotched ground. In designing, the painting of a color background around motifs. In printing, the coloring of a background by printing it with a separate roller or screen.

burnishing. The process of transferring the

backing outline onto the ground paper by rubbing with a spoon.

color-balancing. During designing or printing, the adjustment of color properties to make colors appear as intended when adjacent to each other.

coloring. A painted section of a design in a set of new colors, different from those of the original design.

color properties. Characteristics of color: hue, value, and intensity.

colorway. One printed coloring of a printed design. Designs usually come in several different colorways.

color weight. The tint or shade of a color.

converter. A company that buys greige goods and converts them into printed fabric. Converting houses style print lines, arrange for the printing and finishing of greige fashions, and sell completed cloth to manufacturers and others.

croquis. A drawn and/or painted sketch for a printed textile design.

cross grain. The horizontal threads (weft) of a woven textile.

density. The rate of proximity of recurring motifs or design elements within the layout.

design direction. The look or theme expressed by a group of textile designs.

design in repeat. Refers to the croquis, once it has been developed into a unit and organized by the offset or aligned system.

direct printing. Any printing process in which color is applied directly to the fabric. Roller printing with pigment is an example of direct printing.

discharge printing. A method of printing in which the design is bleached out of a dyed base cloth and another color is simultaneously replaced in the bleached areas.

doctor blade. In roller printing, a blade that scrapes excess color from the engraved roller.

drawing compass. A drawing tool, usually used for drawing circles and arcs, which can also be adapted for other uses.

dye. In textile printing, a coloring agent that is absorbed by the fibers.

engineered print. A printed fabric designed to be cut apart and made into predetermined articles, such as towels, tablecloths, or bedsheets.

engraving sketch. The croquis developed into repeat. It is a facsimile on paper of the way the design will look when repeated on cloth.

finishing. The process through which the fabric is taken after printing, including brushing, glazing, heat-setting, and a variety of chemical processes that change the fabric's feel and look.

frisket. A resist method on paper in which areas of the background are blocked out to repel color during painting.

flush-joining. A joining technique by which two pieces of paper can be inlaid into each other.

gouache. A water base, opaque paint, mixed with a gum preparation; frequently used in creating printed textile designs.

greige goods. Raw fabric in its unfinished state.

ground paper. The surface on which the design is painted.

halftones. The gradations of one color from light to dark that can be printed by the same roller or screen.

hue. In color theory, the identifying name placing a particular color on the spectrum.

intensity. In color theory, the brightness or dullness of a color.

layout. The preliminary composition of the croquis or repeat; usually done on tracing paper.

layout direction. In a printed textile design, the position of the motifs in relation to the selvage. Prints are either one-directional, two-directional, or multi-directional.

length repeat. See repeat unit length.

manufacturer. A company that buys printed fabrics to produce finished products, such as dresses or upholstered furniture. Some manufacturers buy designs in croquis form and have them produced on fabric by a converting house.

mercerizing. A treatment in which cotton or linen is immersed in a caustic soda solution, causing permanent swelling of the fiber and increasing its luster, strength, and dye affinity.

motif. A recurring design element in a croquis.

negative space. The background of the design; not part of the motif.

offset repeat. The system of positioning interlocking repeat units so that they are aligned vertically, but offset, or shifted, horizontally.

pigment. In textile printing a coloring agent which affixes to the surface of the fabric.

positive space. All areas of a design that are not background; for example, the area that a motif occupies is positive space.

printing. A surface process for producing a design on textiles.

print paste. Thickened dye or pigment used in printing.

repeat. The organization of the design elements of the croquis into units that recur at constant intervals, according to a system.

repeat system. The arrangement of interlocking units in aligned or offset repeat. (See *aligned repeat* and *offset repeat*.)

repeat unit. The basic unit of organization within the repeat system consisting of all design elements contained in the croquis.

repeat unit length. The length of the repeat unit. It can never be longer than the circumference of the roller or screen. In flat-bed printing, it cannot exceed the screen length.

repeat unit width. The width of the repeat unit. It may be a few inches or the total width of the roller or screen.

repeated motif. A design element that appears in the same position in each repeat unit.

roller printing. A mechanical process of printing textiles with a series of engraved rollers.

rotary-screen printing. A process in which cylindrical screens are used to apply color to fabric.

rub-down. The transfer of the traced layout backing by burnishing onto ground paper.

ruling pen. A tool filled with gouache or ink and used to draw thin, accurate lines.

selvage. The edge on either side of the fabric, woven to prevent raveling.

side repeat. The repeat of the unit horizontally across the cloth.

squeegee. In screen printing, a rubber blade that moves color and forces it onto the fabric.

step and repeat. A photographic process in which a single repeat-unit, which has been color-separated on clear acetate sheets, is extended to the full width and circumference of the roller or screen used in printing.

stippling. A method of producing a fine, speckled effect on paper; similar to air brush.

straight grain. The vertical threads (warp) of a woven textile.

strike-off. A sample swatch consisting of several repeat lengths of fabric printed on the Saueressig machine before the design goes into production. The strike-off is used to check the accurate translation of the design onto rollers or screens and to establish color looks.

stylist. The creative director in a converter's design studio, responsible for the development of designs and color looks; often oversees the printing of the fabric.

Sublistatic. Another name for transfer printing.

textile. A woven fabric.

transfer printing. A method of printing in which the design is first printed on coated paper and later transferred onto the cloth by use of heat and pressure.

value. In color theory, the lightness or darkness of a color.

Bibliography

ALBERS, JOSEPH. *Interaction of Color.* New Haven: Yale University Press, 1971.

BIRREN, FABER. *Principles of Color.* New York: Van Nostrand Reinhold Company, 1969.

CRAWFORD, TAD. *Legal Guide for the Visual Artist.* New York: Hawthorn Books, Inc., 1977.

Decorattivo 1. Editorial board of Centro Design Montefiber. Milan, Italy: Cassell & Collier Macmillian Publishers, Ltd., 1976.

Encyclopedia of Textiles. Editors of American Fabrics Magazine. Englewood Cliffs, N.J.: Prentice-Hall, Inc., 1972.

The Graphic Artists Guild Handbook: Pricing and Ethical Guide Lines, Fourth Edition. Editorial board of the Graphic Artists Guild. New York: Graphic Artists Guild, 1981.

JOSEPH, MARJORY L. *Introductory Textile Science, Fourth Edition.* New York: Holt, Rinehart and Winston, 1981.

LARSEN, JACK LENOR AND JEANNE WEEKS. *Fabrics for Interiors.* New York: Van Nostrand Reinhold Company, 1975.

LAUER, DAVID A. *Design Basics.* New York: Holt, Rinehart and Winston, 1979.

WARD, MICHAEL. *Art and Design in Textiles.* London: Van Nostrand Reinhold Company, 1975.

Index